LEADING THROUGH Uncertainty

LEADING THROUGH Uncertainty

How UMPQUA BANK Emerged from the Great Recession BETTER AND STRONGER THAN EVER

Ray Davis With PETER ECONOMY

Foreword by William C. Taylor

JOSSEY-BASS™
A Wiley Brand

Design concept by Gearbox
Cover photograph by Vito Palmisano | Getty

Published by Jossey-Bass
A Wiley Imprint

One Montgomery Street, Suite 1200, San Francisco, CA 94104-4594—www.josseybass.com

Jossey-Bass books and products are available through most bookstores. To contact
Jossey-Bass directly call our Customer Care Department within the U.S. at 800-956-7739,
outside the U.S. at 317-572-3986, or fax 317-572-4002.

Wiley publishes in a variety of print and electronic formats and by print-on-demand. Some
material included with standard print versions of this book may not be included in e-books or
in print-on-demand. If this book refers to media such as a CD or DVD that is not included
in the version you purchased, you may download this material at http://booksupport.
wiley.com. For more information about Wiley products, visit www.wiley.com.

Library of Congress Cataloging-in-Publication Data

Davis, Ray, date
    Leading through uncertainty : how Umpqua Bank emerged from the Great
Recession better and stronger than ever / Raymond P. Davis.—First edition.
        pages cm
    Includes index.
    ISBN 978-1-118-73302-8 (hardback)—ISBN 978-1-118-78257-6 (pdf)—ISBN
978-1-118-78260-6 (epub)
        1. Umpqua Bank.   2. Community banks—Oregon—Portland—
Management.   3. Banks and banking—Oregon—Portland—Management.
4. Leadership.   I. Title.
HG2613.P84U473   2014
332.1'609797—dc23

                                                                    2013027869

Printed in the United States of America
FIRST EDITION

HB Printing   10 9 8 7 6 5 4 3 2 1

Contents

PART 3
LEADING THE WAY

For the associates of Umpqua Bank.
You lead, you motivate, and you inspire.

Foreword

More than a century ago, Theodore Roosevelt offered a definition of success that has stood the test of time. "Far and away the best prize that life offers," he said, "is the chance to work hard at work worth doing." By that definition, Ray Davis is one of the most successful business leaders I have ever met. He and his colleagues at Umpqua Bank have worked harder, smarter, and with more passion and authenticity than the leadership of any other bank I know—and, to be honest, just about any organization in any field that I know. And their work is certainly worth doing—building a company, a brand, a presence in the marketplace that stands out from the crowd and stands for something special.

Leading Through Uncertainty is Ray's second effort to share with the world (with all his trademark modesty) what he and his colleagues have learned during their incredible twenty-year journey of innovation, service, and exceptional financial performance. His first book, *Leading for Growth*, was published in March 2007, when the banking business, and the world economy as a whole, were riding high and enjoying the tailwinds of housing booms and fast-paced growth. His new book appears at a very different moment in the economy and in the psychology that animates leaders and shapes their outlook. Most companies in most industries, and certainly in the banking industry, are operating in the face of fierce headwinds—the hangover from the worst financial collapse since the Great Depression, frustratingly slow growth in the real economy, a hard-to-shake sense of distrust between customers and the companies with which they do business.

And yet the Ray Davis you will encounter in these pages, the Umpqua Bank that he and his writing colleague, Peter Economy, bring to life, is every bit as confident, every bit as passionate, every bit as daring as was the case during the height of the boom. That's because even as the world changes—as the Internet and social media reinvent the technologies of banking, as financial trends and government policies reshape the environment of banking—Ray and his colleagues have remained true to their values, their belief system, their distinctive point of view about what their company could be and the role it could play in their customers' lives.

In a book filled with powerful insights, pragmatic takeaways, and colorful stories, this to me is Ray's ultimate lesson, and one that applies in good times and tough times. He understands, as few other CEOs do, that we are living today through the Age of Disruption. You can't do big things anymore, as a company or a leader, if you are content with doing things a little better than everybody else, or a little differently from how you did them in the past. In an era of hypercompetition and nonstop dislocation, the only way to stand out from the crowd is to stand for something special. Originality has become the acid test of every company's strategy.

The term I like to use is *strategy as advocacy*—and Ray and his colleagues are persuasive advocates for their approach to strategy. They understand that the most successful companies don't just offer competitive products and services. They champion compelling ideas—ideas that shape the competitive landscape of their field, ideas that reshape the sense of what's possible for customers, for colleagues, for investors. As I look at companies that are winning big in difficult circumstances, I see that a richly defined values proposition beats a dollars-and-cents value proposition every time.

To be sure, no one will mistake Umpqua Bank for one of the financial services juggernauts headquartered in New York or Hong Kong, and no one will mistake Ray himself for a Master of the Universe or a Titan of Finance. And that's the beauty of this book. Ray's insights and messages are worth reckoning with not because of the size of his bank's balance sheet (although all those billions of dollars of assets are beginning to add up), but because of the power of his ideas and their relevance to many leaders running companies in many different industries.

For a long time, we lived in a world where the strong took from the weak. If you had the most established brand, the widest global reach, the deepest pockets, you won almost automatically. That world is over. The new logic of success is that the smart take from the strong. The most successful companies I have gotten to know don't just try to outcompete their rivals. They aspire to redefine the terms of competition in their field by embracing one-of-a-kind ideas in a world filled with me-too, copycat thinking. In Ray's memorable words, these companies "find the revolution before the revolution finds them."

Ideas truly matter. But there's a second core message to Ray's book, a second defining principle of his approach to leadership, that it's important to underscore. It's a lesson I've learned and relearned during this long economic crisis—and even though it's a simple lesson, it's one that's all too easy to overlook. Yes, the most successful leaders and companies think differently from everyone else. But they also care more than everybody else— about customers, about colleagues, about how the organization conducts itself in a world with endless opportunities to cut corners and compromise on values. You can't be special, distinctive, compelling in the marketplace unless you create something special, distinctive, compelling in the workplace. Your strategy *is* your culture; your culture *is* your strategy. That's why the most effective leaders serve an agenda larger than themselves and create organizations where everyone shares a common cause.

This, to me, is what ultimately makes Ray Davis and Umpqua Bank so special. Ray is a CEO, and Umpqua is a company of more than twenty-five hundred people who care deeply about the impact they're having, the legacy they're leaving, the difference they're making in the lives of their customers and communities. It is also, by the way, what makes this book so special. Ray obviously cares enough about what he and his colleagues have built to share the lessons they've learned, the successes they've enjoyed, and the mistakes they've made with an audience of leaders who are working hard inside their own companies on work worth doing.

Thanks to Ray for sharing his insights, and good luck to all of you benefiting from it as you pursue, in the words of Theodore Roosevelt, "the best prize that life offers."

William C. Taylor
cofounder and founding editor of *Fast Company*
and author of *Practically Radical*

Introduction:
The Great Uncertainty

Much of the world is stuck in the economic doldrums, a place where there is precious little breeze to push the weathervane in any particular direction. Is the economy headed toward growth and prosperity, or is an even bigger recession just around the corner? Will this be the year that unemployment rates finally return to manageable levels, or are the increasing ranks of people who have dropped out of the job market entirely going to be a heavy anchor that keeps our economy from moving forward? Is there an inflationary (or deflationary) spiral in our not-too-distant future?

When will things get back to normal? Will they *ever* get back to normal?

I call this time in history the Great Uncertainty, and it's the place where we find ourselves today. No one really knows with any degree of confidence where our economy is headed and whether the general business environment will be better or worse in the coming months or years. I personally believe that the uncomfortable new normal of uncertainty we find ourselves in today is a long-term reality that business leaders will be forced to deal with for at least the next five years. To succeed, we as leaders cannot afford to complain about the uncertainty out there—in our economy, our markets, our government representatives and regulators, our customers, our people. We must instead find ways to deal with this new normal, and to profit, even during the Great Uncertainty.

We must be leaders. We must *lead*.

My first book, *Leading for Growth*, was published in late 2007, before the 2007 financial crisis had taken hold of the economy. While I was writing that book, the U.S. economy was strong and growing, the housing market was seen by many as indestructible (or at least indefatigable), and consumer confidence was as high as it had ever been. *Leading for Growth* was written to offer a fresh look at how leaders could steer their companies to long-term success. That book offered tools and techniques that could be embraced by all people who found themselves in a leadership role. *Leading for Growth* didn't take an MBA to understand or put into practice. It was a down-to-earth reminder of the basic leadership tenets that have proven year after year to be effective in leading a company for growth.

Throughout the book, I provided examples of how leaders have put these skills to work within their companies. As the CEO of Umpqua Holdings Corporation, the holding company for Umpqua Bank, a regional community bank headquartered in Portland, Oregon, I was also able to relate specific stories of how Umpqua benefited from many of these leadership principles. Although I often used Umpqua Bank to demonstrate how we applied these practices, *Leading for Growth* was written for all leaders in all industries, and I heard from many executives both inside and outside the banking industry who put them to work.

As we look back to the period leading up to the onset of the Great Recession, the effects of which still negatively affect the world today, who would have thought that our economy would fall as far as it did? Who would have thought that the housing market would drop as fast as it did and affect so many Americans so dramatically? Who would have thought that our problems would become contagious and affect the economy throughout the rest of the world?

Few people imagined just how bad things would get or how long it would take to recover. However, one thing was certain throughout: effective leadership during difficult times is not only needed; it is *required*.

Leading Through Uncertainty addresses just that: the importance of leadership within organizations competing during challenging and uncertain times—and also through times of growth. Let's face it: effective leadership is motivating, and it can and should be the energy that propels a company through inevitable waves of change. Poor leadership can lead to disaster and has sunk more than a few companies and governments alike.

In *Leading for Growth* I wrote, "There is no Door Number 3." I meant that leaders have to be willing to address, accept, and welcome change instead of fighting it, ignoring it, or simply hoping it will go away. Change happens, and trying to stay the same isn't practical: it's too costly and is an impossible proposition. I believe that this still applies for leaders. You have to be ready and able to adapt to rapid changes during times of great difficulty and uncertainty—and also during times of great innovation or growth. It also means that when things get tough, a leader can either choose Door Number One (meaning, suck it up and do what you know you need to do—*lead*), or choose Door Number Two (meaning, get the hell out of the way!). There is no Door Number Three.

Although Umpqua wasn't immune to economic turmoil, we were disciplined and proactive, and that approach served us well. We identified potential challenges early and took action immediately—before most other companies had even acknowledged that the economy was in trouble. Although our bold response wasn't popular on Wall Street at the time, it positioned the bank as one of the most stable in the industry.

Throughout, we remained focused on both navigating the recession and our long-term growth strategy. Despite the challenging economic environment, that strategy never wavered. We remained focused on building a different kind of bank—one that combines the sophisticated products and expertise of a big bank with the service and local engagement of a community bank. This allowed us to remain opportunistic in ways that advanced our growth. During this time, we completed four transactions assisted by the Federal Deposit Insurance Corporation (FDIC), adding significantly to our geographic reach while protecting the financial health of communities in Nevada and Washington State.

And we were able to act quickly when we saw the economic storm beginning to calm, expanding our company in ways that would build for the future. We added wealth management, international banking, and capital markets divisions; expanded our commercial teams in key markets; and built new stores to complement those acquired through the FDIC deals.

As a result, Umpqua's balance sheet today is even stronger than it was when the financial crisis began. And we've continued to grow, nearly doubling in size since 2007, from 120 to more than 200 stores and from $7 billion to $12 billion in assets.

* * *

Over the past several years, I've learned firsthand the power of strong leadership. In this book, I outline qualities that leaders need to motivate and inspire their people in times of change, both to protect their businesses when market conditions are difficult and to build confidence and momentum in times of positive change.

Leading Through Uncertainty reminds leaders to:

- Remember that the truth will set them free.

- Remain agile in the face of uncertainty and change.

- Keep their heads out of the sand when problems arise.

- Understand the value of intuition and why it's important for their people to exercise theirs.

- Motivate and inspire their people in order to build successful companies.

- Recognize the need for momentum and the value of leverage.

- Build a company culture that reinforces a meaningful value proposition.

Problems don't normally evaporate without leadership, and by understanding and practicing basic leadership principles, leaders can successfully navigate their companies through even the roughest water. Like *Leading for Growth*, this book is a conversation on leadership rather than a how-to manual. In my first book, I wrote about the nature of change and how it encourages us to think of leadership in a new way. As we slowly leave the Great Recession further behind and work our way through the Great Uncertainty, this book takes those who understand the challenges of leadership during difficult times and urges them to practice their skills and apply them for the benefit of their people, their customers, their organizations, and their communities.

Leading Through Uncertainty is divided into three parts: Leading Yourself, Leading Your Organization, and Leading Your Industry. Each part explores an essential aspect of leadership practice. You can't be a truly effective leader without becoming proficient in each of these areas of leadership practice.

Part 1, "Leading Yourself," is about how a leader has to get comfortable within his or her own skin in order to lead others effectively. In other words, how confident are you, the leader, in yourself? It shouldn't be difficult, but unfortunately all too often it's painful for leaders to be truthful with both themselves and with fellow workers. We frequently read stories in the news about leaders who are obviously avoiding the truth, timing an announcement, or trying to soften the blow to others when full disclosure is the best course of action for their people and organizations. Believe me: being truthful will absolutely set you free. By being forthright and transparent, you will gain respect and credibility from others, while reinforcing your own leadership ability. In addition to exploring the value of being truthful and the energizing impact it can have on organizations, the chapters in Part 1 consider:

- How accepting the fact that the new normal isn't normal at all can help get leaders past the "hesitation machine" and propel them to seek out changes that are fast approaching

- Why leaders should worry only about the issues that they and their people can control, yet be ready to deal with the uncertainty that's all around us

- The negative impact that discounting the impact of intangibles like intuition can have on an organization

Part 2, "Leading Your Organization," takes the personal leadership skills of the leader outward, to the company and the organization. The chapters in this part explore how important the perception of the leader and the company within the organization may be, while recognizing how that perception others have can become truth. The strong leader will never discount this fact. This part explores a number of topics:

- The value of being really good at executing the basic underlying fundamentals of a business.
- The creation of a meaningful value proposition, which can set you apart from your competition and propel your company forward.
- What being available to all of your many different stakeholders can mean to the organization and the influence this has on sustaining a company in times of great turbulence and uncertainty.
- The simple fact that leaders can't lead if they can't motivate and inspire their people. There are many ways to accomplish this, and it is a leader's job to figure out what approaches are most effective.
- How, even in difficult times, a leader must have the vision to know when to leverage up a company's assets.

The first two parts of this book aim to prepare leaders to accomplish great things for themselves and for their people. The chapters in Part 3, "Leading the Way," offer strong fundamental strategies that can lead to progressive advances within your company, propelling it to the top of its industry.

As I wrote in *Leading for Growth*, all businesspeople have a common mission: to get clients and customers to shop with them. All business leaders are hard at work trying to discover the recipe for the secret sauce that will differentiate their company or business from their competition. It's a simple fact that we're all trying to accomplish this and that it's an all-consuming job. The four chapters in this part address:

- How a company's reputation is one of its greatest—and most vulnerable—assets. If it's not tended to properly, even the best reputation can erode and cause serious issues for the organization.

- How to take a company's value proposition and inspire others to turbocharge it, while constantly evolving to keep your company fresh and its competitive gap alive.

- Knowing when to pull back and when to start building momentum for the future.

- How to differentiate your business from others that are selling the same products or services.

Leading Through Uncertainty is a practical book of commonsense advice that will help leaders in any business and any industry sustain their company through uncertain economic times. This isn't a book of science or formulas, and it's not a book about obscure management practices. This is a book about leadership, pure and simple, from the perspective of someone who has successfully guided a company through great challenges. Above all, this is a book of common sense that I hope will resonate with readers and bring to life those essential leadership skills that we all need to be reminded of from time to time.

I have no doubt that there will be many booms and busts in the decades to come; it's a natural part of the global economy, and history is full of both. However, regardless of which direction the winds of economic change eventually blow, the truth is that there is no certainty in either calm or tumultuous waters. If you are a leader, you must be prepared to lead through uncertainty. If you can't or won't lead, then step aside and make room for someone who will, because there is still no Door Number Three.

LEADING THROUGH Uncertainty

Leading Yourself

Control is not leadership; management is not leadership; leadership is leadership. If you seek to lead, invest at least 50 percent of your time in leading yourself—your own purpose, ethics, principles, motivation, conduct. Invest at least 20 percent leading those with authority over you and 15 percent leading your peers.
—Dee Hock, founder and CEO emeritus, Visa

Before you can lead others, you first need to learn how to lead yourself. Leading yourself will help you hone the skills you'll need to lead others, while building the confidence that infuses good leaders and builds the confidence of those they lead. Part 1 considers a number of topics related to self-leadership, including getting your arms around today's headlines, the importance of telling the truth, dealing with problems, understanding what you can and cannot control, and exercising your intuition.

1

The New Normal

Destiny is not a matter of chance; it is a matter of choice. It is
not a thing to be waited for, it is a thing to be achieved.
—William Jennings Bryan

The effects of the global financial crisis continue to affect
our economy: growth and unemployment rates haven't
yet stabilized, and change is constant and faster than ever
before. We're in the new normal—a time when there *is* no
normal. Now more than ever before, leaders must be looking
over the horizon to the next revolution—before it overtakes
their businesses and their customers along with it.

Since my book *Leading for Growth* was published in 2007, the
world has been through an economic tsunami that has wrought
incredible damage. Although Umpqua Bank, a regional community bank headquartered in Portland, Oregon, has done well
in these uncertain times, other companies—and the citizens of
many countries—haven't been so lucky. The economic recovery
that followed the 2007–2009 recession has been particularly
weak due to many factors, including a stubbornly high unemployment rate, the impact of European fiscal disasters, and the

ineffectiveness of Congress to address the major issues facing the United States, to name just a few. The impact of the recession, coupled with a slow and uncertain recovery, has left many families and businesses bruised and battered, resulting in an American public that for good reason is worried about the future.

We're stuck in a kind of economic no-man's-land where anything can and just might happen. Is a double-dip recession waiting for us a few months down the road? Maybe. It's not out of the question. A boom driven by a sudden surge in consumer demand? Sure. It's a possibility if consumer confidence begins to rise. Even the things that we have long taken for granted—fully stocked grocery stores, lights that work when you flip the switch, and water that flows from the tap when you turn it on—may soon be at risk according to experts who point out that the infrastructure of post–World War II America is wearing out.[1]

Of course, this new normal isn't all negative. Out of this economic trial by fire, we're seeing great creativity and innovation in technology and business, which is resulting in remarkable new products and services that are produced more efficiently than ever before. Entrepreneurs are starting up new businesses at a high rate. According to the Kauffman Foundation in Kansas City, Missouri, more than 500,000 new business owners were minted in the United States each month in 2013.[2]

Nevertheless, the uncertainty of the times we're in—and can expect to be in for many years into the future—creates anxiety and fear, and this anxiety and fear drive the decisions that we make. Let's face it: When we are scared, confused, and worried about our prospects, we all have a tendency to do nothing and hope the storm passes over us without too much damage, or we overreact impulsively—sometimes exacerbating the bad situation we are already experiencing.

We business leaders are no different from the people we lead. We often feel compelled to take action in difficult or uncertain times. Sometimes we do this to make a difference when we see a clear path to our goals, and sometimes we do this just to let people know that we're awake at the wheel. Business leaders are human, and we often find ourselves in situations where our fellow associates are looking for and expecting us to remain calm and deliberate—and we overreact. In the heat of the battle, it's natural for leaders to overreact to the conditions in which they find themselves instead of staying calm and acting only when necessary. The old saying "It's better to do something than to do nothing" isn't always the best advice to follow. In fact, in many cases, doing something for the sake of appearing busy—or what has been described as "firing for effect"—can get you and your company into even deeper trouble than if you had instead done nothing.

I have to wonder whether Netflix's decision in 2011 to split its business into two—creating one company, Qwikster, that would handle its legacy DVD rental business and another company, retaining the original Netflix name, that would be responsible for the online video streaming business—was an overreaction to fast-changing and uncertain market conditions. The net result for Netflix's loyal customers was twofold. First, the price they would pay for their Netflix subscriptions would double overnight, from a minimum of $7.99 a month to $15.98 a month. In addition, those same customers would also have to deal with two companies to get the same services they were getting from the original Netflix. This led to a virtual riot among Netflix customers that aggressively built momentum through newly popular social media channels, with 16 percent reporting soon after the decision went public that they would cancel their subscriptions.

The result? The price of shares of Netflix stock sunk 57 percent in just two months, and the plan was scuttled by company founder Reed Hastings before it went into effect. Said Hastings at the time, "There is a difference between moving quickly—which Netflix has done very well for years—and moving too fast, which is what we did in this case."[3]

The dilemma we often find ourselves in during uncertain times is made more complicated by the simple fact that it's almost impossible to remain the same. It has long been said that there are only two things we can count on in life: taxes and death. We need to add one more certainty to that short list: change. But unlike the other two, change can be exciting, positive, and rewarding.

It's interesting to watch how people react to the simple expression "We are going to make changes," or "If we are going to improve, we need to change," or any of the many other ways of saying the same thing. I'm sure there are many psychologists and physiologists who would point out that we are genetically programmed at an early age to fear and worry about change. Indeed, according to experts in organization change, more than 70 percent of all organization change efforts fail, and failed change is the number 1 reason that business leaders get fired.[4] Much of the blame for these failures can be traced to the resistance to change that seems to be genetically wired into many of us. I often wonder why this is so when change can be so inspiring. If you don't believe change can be beautiful, just watch your children grow.

In business, change is a constant, and its velocity is getting faster and faster. According to Harvard Business School professor John Kotter, "Rate of change in the world today is going up. It's going up fast, and it's affecting organizations in a huge way. And what's particularly important is that it's not just going up. It's increasingly going up not just in a linear slant, but almost exponentially."[5]

Just when you think you have something figured out, new technologies or systems are created to change things. Again. The simple fact is you can't stay the same. Although it's challenging for organizations to embrace change, staying the same is even costlier and more difficult. Even better, of course, is to get out in front of coming changes in your business environment and to anticipate and respond to them before they arrive.

Suppose you're driving on the freeway at fifty-five miles per hour. How difficult is it to keep that speed constant versus slowing down or speeding up? (For the troublemakers reading this, yes, that assumes you can't use cruise control.) The point here is simple: you *will* change, and it's up to you how you are going to make the transition. You can adapt to change because you "have to" or because and when you "want to." The choice is up to you. Pick one.

Change comes in all sizes and levels of importance, can affect budgets, and usually shows up, or at least so it seems, at the most inopportune times. This we can count on. What's important is how we respond and react to change.

We can embrace change knowing we have no other choice, or we can overreact or panic, causing havoc within our companies. If we choose to be proactive about change, we must actively "hunt" for it and try to prevent it from making surprise visits. This is productive, positive, and powerful. The decision to freeze up or overreact to difficult situations or changes that are forced on us is counterproductive, morale killing, and the start of death spirals in many companies. These two polar opposite reactions to challenges and crises in the business environment are counterdirectional, and different leaders often act in sometimes completely different ways in response to the same events. While some are ready to anticipate change and "lead the revolution" when it arrives, others see change coming, panic, and stick their heads in the sand.

Which kind of leader are you? Which kind of leader do you want to be? If you're not the kind of leader you want to be, how will you change to meet this challenge, and when will you do it?

A WORLD IN FLUX

By definition, a *revolution* is a complete and radical change in something, and a *panic* is a sudden, overwhelming fear that produces hysterical behavior. A revolution is change put into practice, while panic is an irrational and emotional reaction to that change. Panic can quickly spread throughout an organization, causing widespread fear and concerns if it isn't quickly addressed and defeated. As you can well imagine, panic is rarely (if ever) a good thing for any company. In virtually every case I've seen over the years, panic creates hysterical, unproductive behavior among a company's people that leads to bad decisions and lousy results. And we are not in business to provide lousy results—to our customers, our associates, or our shareholders.

Revolutions occur all the time in the world around us. While the word *revolution* most often makes us think of countries engaged in political upheavals, revolutions also impact the world of business and the consumers of their products and services. I think it's reasonable to believe that the radical changes we experience in all types of industries can rise to meet the definition of a revolution. Consider the introduction of the first cell phone, the first personal computer, the first heart transplant, the first satellite placed in orbit around the earth, and any number of other product advances that have radically changed our lives for the better. These events were profound when they occurred, but it's what they created that is so critical.

Business revolutions of this magnitude are still happening today with no slowdown in sight. Reading glasses of various strengths are produced in China at a cost of less than fifty cents a pair. This advance has the potential to affect the lives of more than 100 million people around the globe who have trouble reading close up. European utility companies are exploring the replacement of coal with briquettes made from sustainable timber by-products, including sawdust and tree bark. Considering that 6 billion tons of coal are burned worldwide each year, rapidly depleting the world's supplies of this key fossil fuel resource, a revolutionary advance of this magnitude could have a huge and lasting impact on our ability to power the future.[6]

Revolutions, however, do not have to be big to be important; they don't require a radical transformation of the world as we know it to have a big impact. Sometimes it's the small revolutions that can make big differences in how we live and conduct business.

The introduction of FedEx is a great example. This small start-up company founded by Frederick Smith in 1971 created a revolution in package delivery. Before FedEx took off, getting documents to a distant destination overnight was a difficult and cost-prohibitive proposition. FedEx (which once marketed itself as "a freight service company with 550-mile-per-hour delivery trucks") completely changed the paradigm, making overnight delivery of envelopes and packages a routine, reliable, and relatively inexpensive event.[7] While the company today is one of the world's largest and most successful businesses (ranked number seventy in the Fortune 500, the company has annual revenues of more than $42 billion and operates a fleet of almost seven hundred aircraft and more than fifty thousand delivery vehicles and trailers), it started out with just a handful of airplanes Smith acquired when he purchased a used aircraft company in Little Rock, Arkansas, in 1971.[8] A small revolution in the transportation industry gave birth to something much bigger.

Revolutions can be opportunities to be taken advantage of, or they can be disruptions that cripple our ability to carry on with our existing business paradigm. They can be positive and inspiring if we find them before they find us, or they can be devastating and destructive if they find us first.

I see revolutions and opportunities as synonymous. A revolution or opportunity discovered early can be awe inspiring, while a revolution or opportunity that passes you by—only to return and snap you hard on the side of the head—can be troubling, to say the least. You should always be looking for revolutions, but it's important to remember that sometimes they're not as obvious as you expect them to be, and they don't usually announce their arrival. Revolutions may remain under the radar and take time to gather momentum before they take hold. But whether you notice them or not, they're there.

When I talk about revolutions with executives from other banks, I tell them that they should be very worried that the revolution doesn't find them first. The history of business is paved with the wreckage of companies that were run over by revolutions they didn't see coming: Eastman Kodak (photographic film and film cameras, overtaken by digital photography), Bethlehem Steel (steel, pushed aside by less-expensive and better-quality foreign steel imports), and Blockbuster (video rental, made obsolete by Netflix and other online DVD rental and then video-streaming companies).

We've similarly experienced a revolution in banking over the past decade or so. A lot of people in the United States don't physically go to their bank branches anymore. Instead, they do the vast majority of their banking—from paying bills, to checking balances and transferring funds, and even depositing checks using the camera in a smart phone—at home. And those few things they can't do at home, like making cash deposits and withdrawals, they can now accomplish at an ATM at their bank or in a mall or grocery store or gas station. (There's even an ATM in Las Vegas's Golden Nugget Hotel & Casino that dispenses .9999 pure gold instead of cash.⁹) Today there's very little reason for you to actually go to a bank for anything.

That's a revolution, and for those of us in the banking industry, it's a complete and total game changer. But it's also been a long time coming.

With this revolution came huge challenges for our industry. I can tell you that the best opportunities for bankers to create and build relationships with prospective and existing customers is not through a web page where people can quickly shop for the best rates and then sign off.

Banking is a relationship business, meaning we're only as good as our people are. Therefore, the answer to where we're best able to build relationships with prospective and existing customers is in a bank, when they're face-to-face with a real person. That's where personal relationships are built, not through a computer and an online banking website.

But wait a minute—we have a dilemma here. Bank customers are by choice using bank branches less often, yet that's where most of our new accounts are opened and relationships built. Our industry is currently confronted with a difficult problem—one resulting from a revolution. The revolution we're facing is the result of advancing technology and evolving customer preferences, changes that have been in the works for decades. If we aren't able to adapt, we will suffer the consequences. The challenge is this: How do we evolve the function of bank branches in ways that make them relevant and enable us to continue to expand our businesses?

At Umpqua, we recognized years ago as consumer technology was just beginning to evolve that differentiating ourselves from the competition would be one of the biggest challenges we would face as a company. This challenge is the same one that every business today confronts. Every company in the world is trying to figure this out by asking, "Why should you shop with me?" In our case, banks offer pretty much the same interest rates for deposits and loans, and we all provide checking and savings accounts. In order to show that we offer better value than our competitors, we need to create opportunities for our associates to engage with our customers. The relationships developed through personal interaction are powerful, and they have tremendous value to our customers—so much so that they may be willing to ignore the fact that another bank down the street is paying a little more interest on its deposits this week or has a nicer lobby or parking lot.

Often the customers who shop for electronics on the Internet first go to their local mom-and-pop shop or even one of the larger big-box chains such as Best Buy, Costco, or Walmart to do research about their purchase. They'll talk the ears off a sales associate to get detailed information about the item they want to buy and narrow down their choices to the best one or two products. And then they hurry home, jump on their computer, and buy the item from Amazon.com. The customer has taken advantage of all the overhead their local stores are paying for and then made their final decision based on price—bypassing the very stores that are employing their family, friends, and neighbors and instead sending their money to some far-away destination. To add insult to injury, they may not be paying sales tax on the transaction either, shorting their state and local governments at the same time.

Unfortunately this could be the way of the world from now on. It is up to leaders to recognize this reality and respond accordingly. And the time to act is now. Any business that fails to create a value proposition that's specifically designed to capture the interest of potential customers and give them a compelling reason to consider something besides just price in the buying equation could be writing its own obituary.

That's the revolution occurring in business now, and we either respond to it or the revolution runs us over. At Umpqua we responded to this revolution as an opportunity, and in a way you might not expect.

CHANGE THE GAME

Instead of shutting down our existing locations and putting plans for new ones on ice, we decided years ago that bank branches would still be important; however, they're going to have to evolve—but we were going to have to *make* them important— and do it quickly and totally. That's where we started back in the late 1990s when we designed and built our very first bank store. We don't have bank branches at Umpqua; all of our branches have been redesigned as bank stores. They're inviting places where you can stop in for a while, browse the Internet on one of our public computers, have a cup of our special Umpqua coffee, or grab a cookie. And while you're there, if you happen to want to do your banking, you can do that too.

We try to give people a reason to come into our stores for something other than a traditional banking transaction. On any given afternoon there might be a yoga class going on, or a bowling league playing on a Nintendo Wii console, or a book club, or an art show. Our stores have become community centers, play and social spaces, places where people want to go. This strategy and response to the revolution in banking has allowed us to continue to increase our business even during uncertain times. It's the revolution we've led in the banking industry and one in which we continue to do everything we can to stay out ahead of—to stay a step in front of our competitors, many of whom have tried to copy our innovations with limited degrees of success.

The old-style bank branch where you've got tellers on one side and desks with loan officers at the other—and a velvet rope telling people where they're supposed to stand—is over. It's a formula that's seriously outdated and an example of how other banks are letting the current revolution in the banking industry run over them.

Another revolution gaining a lot of momentum lately is in the health care industry. Eric Topol, a cardiologist at Scripps Health in San Diego, is leading a revolution in the emerging practice of wireless medicine. Using a $199 AliveCor heart monitoring iPhone app, Dr. Topol can obtain the same diagnostic information about his patients—heart rhythm, blood pressure, body temperature, real-time heartbeat, and more—as he can using a far more expensive standard twelve-lead electrocardiograph machine. And using a small handheld ultrasound device, the GE Vscan, which has a retail price of just $7,900,

Dr. Topol can easily and inexpensively image the inside of patients' hearts. This is less than one-fifth the price of a typical medical office ultrasound unit, which can cost $45,000 or more. According to Dr. Topol, he's actually prescribing more cell phone apps to his patients than he is medicine. Talk about a revolution!

While Dr. Topol is considered a bit of a maverick in the medical community, he's on to something. There's a revolution going on in health care that's long overdue. This revolution is being led by advances in technology like those cited above and by risk takers like Dr. Topol—men and women who are leading this revolution and are changing business models and people's lives in the process.

The next revolution is coming. You can't change its course, and you can't stop it. So what's your decision? Are you going to lead it, or are you going to hide from it?

If you're nervous about an emerging revolution in your industry, try to remember that revolutions can provide a remarkable opportunity to advance your company and get well ahead of your competition. Instead of freezing up or overreacting, embrace the revolution and change your business to put you in a position to lead it. Consider what Starbucks has done for the coffee industry. I guarantee that you can make good coffee at home; you don't *need* to go to Starbucks. So why then do people flock to Starbucks? People love Starbucks because it's a good place to go. The coffee is good, perhaps even excellent. The employees make a point of trying to get to know regular customers—anticipating their orders the moment they walk through the door. There are comfortable chairs to lounge in and tables to do some work if you like, plus free Wi-Fi to connect to the Internet. You might see a neighbor or friend, or you might meet someone new. And together these elements have transformed an industry.

When it comes to revolutions and panics, understand that you as a leader must respond proactively or at least constructively to the potential of a revolution. If you wait, your response could be too late. And if you do nothing, you risk the kind of disruptive panic that can have a negative impact on your people, customers, and other stakeholders for years to come.

BE AGILE—YOU CAN'T STAND STILL

In business, being *agile* can refer to a variety of things. One is the ability to avoid problems while you're in the middle of engaging in some major activity or initiative. Another is to engage fully in necessary preparations before a major disaster hits your organization. Or it could mean being quick to take advantage of opportunities as they arise.

There's a word I really despise, because it slows speed and prevents progress. That word is *bureaucracy*. Bureaucracy limits your agility, and any organization big or small can fall victim to it. In his groundbreaking book on social theory, *Capitalism, Socialism, and Democracy*, economist Joseph Schumpeter pointed out the danger of bureaucratic thinking to organizations:

> The bureaucratic method of transacting business and the moral atmosphere it spreads doubtless often exert a depressing influence on the most active minds. Mainly, this is due to the difficulty, inherent in the bureaucratic machine, of reconciling individual initiative with the mechanics of its working. Often, the machine gives little scope for initiative and much scope for vicious attempts at

smothering it. From this a sense of frustration and of futil-
ity may result which in turn induces a habit of mind that
revels in blighting criticism of the efforts of others.[10]

Bureaucracy is the enemy of change, and it is guaranteed
to limit your organization's ability to adapt quickly to fast-
changing conditions in your markets. Bureaucracy isn't the
result of having ten thousand people working for you. Your
organization can be bureaucratic with only ten employees, or
even fewer. If your organization isn't agile, you could lose a
tremendous opportunity to take advantage of something that
would have been in your favor, but because you weren't quick
enough or agile enough, you missed it. Situations like this are
particularly sad because it's not that you didn't think about
taking proactive action; your company was just unable to act
because it couldn't move quickly enough.

You can't afford to stand still. Changes and revolutions are
coming at you every day. Some people are smart enough to see
them and others aren't, but they *will* arrive. And when they do,
they will affect your organization whether or not you see them
coming. Your business is changing all the time. If it's not technology, it's customer preferences. You have to be constantly on
your toes, actively trying to take advantage of what's going on
around you or at least being aware of it. As I've said before, it
actually costs an organization more to try to stay the same than
it does to get better or get worse.

You can walk into a strong headwind as long as you want, but
if it's blowing hard enough, you won't be able to make progress.
It's going to hold you in place or push you backward. The effort
required of you to continue to walk in a wind of that strength
costs more money, effort, and time than it does if you were to

step to the side and let the wind pass by you. The amount of money, human resources, and productivity that is spent trying to stay the same is much greater than trying to get better or worse. On top of that, it's just plain harder to stay the same.

In *Leading for Growth*, I gave the example of treading water in the deep end of a swimming pool. The long and short of the story was that you can't tread water (which represents staying the same) forever. You can, however, immediately change your situation for the better by simply swimming over to the edge of the pool and getting out. Problem solved!

You've got to be agile. Agility can mean taking advantage of opportunities, but it can also mean deciding *not* to take advantage of something. The point is to be agile enough to have options and sufficient time to act, come up with the answer that best fits your company, and then act on it quickly and effectively.

RELENTLESS PROGRESS IS THE KEY

The old saying "That's the way we've always done it" has gone out the window. There is no conventional wisdom in the new normal; it just does not exist, especially with the speed of change and technology.

At Umpqua Bank, we're constantly trying to evolve our culture and our delivery system. Customer preferences change all the time, which I believe makes conventional wisdom the kiss of death. My own preference is for *unconventional* wisdom, which is why I seldom talk to bank consultants. I prefer to engage with people outside my industry. The unconventional ideas they bring me can give me an advantage over my competition because for the most part, bankers limit themselves to what I call "bank think." They're thinking about what banks do. If you own a tire company, why are you interviewing with a tire consultant when they're going to tell you the same thing they told your competitor down the street?

I ask all my people to make progress every day. That's important both to their personal development and to the organization. And progress can come in many shapes and sizes and forms. It can be, "You know, Ray, I've thought about this big project we were going to start and I've delayed it for two weeks because of X, Y, and Z. It's been well thought out, and I think this is the way we should go." To me that's not a problem; that's progress. By thinking an issue through and weighing the risks associated with it, you've perhaps prevented a problem. I compliment people for that. But make no mistake—it's always important that you know what kind of progress you're making every day.

Once a year we conduct a strategic retreat with our board of directors to confirm the overall direction of the company for the next five years. I also meet with my management team to build consensus on our goals for the upcoming year, which must complement our five-year strategic plan. I believe one great way to measure what you have achieved or what you are going to achieve is to turn your time frame upside down. For example, after you've established your goals, play it back to your group as if the year was just completed. Assume it is December 31 (or whatever your year-end date is), and read back to your team all the goals you set during your discussions as if they were all completed within budget and on time during the year. How does that feel? Was it enough? Were we too aggressive? The answers will become very clear.

I also practice this with my board of directors. I play back the goals and give them an idea of where we will be by the end of the year. I draw a mental picture that if the economy and the world behave and we stay in control of our destiny, then this is what we could look like a year from now. Usually we all feel pretty good about our aspirations for the upcoming year and are confident we will make relentless progress toward achieving them. That's another way to measure progress.

DEAL WITH IT

So, yes, the world is in flux, and revolutions and changes continue to come at us like fireworks exploding in the night sky. For some, these changes, coupled with the ever-increasing speed of evolving technology, are just too much to handle. For others, their companies are not built to sustain damage from economic storms that ultimately create the new normal environment we will be expected to thrive in. However, for those who are willing to embrace change, create a nimble workforce, and look to make progress every day in this new environment, the headwinds might get strong but they will manage to get through it.

"Just Do It" has been Nike's trademarked tagline for more than twenty-five years. In this environment, *my* tagline is, "Just Deal with It."

FOR REFLECTION

- How has the new normal affected your business? You personally?

- What do you do to try to make uncertain times more certain? Are these approaches working for you?

- Is fear of change prevalent in your organization? If so, what are you doing to mitigate it?

- What are you doing to identify coming revolutions in your industry? What are you doing to get ahead of these revolutions?

- In what ways is your industry changing? What are you doing to respond?

2

The Truth, Nothing But the Truth

I am a firm believer in the people. If given the truth, they can
be depended upon to meet any national crisis. The great point
is to bring them the real facts.
—Abraham Lincoln

When times are difficult, uncertainty reigns and employees get nervous. Will they have a job tomorrow? Will
they have a company tomorrow? A leader's job is to tell the
unvarnished truth and rid their organizations of the fear of the
unknown. The news may not always be good, but your people
need to understand what's going on so they can deal with it.

Some people think of the truth in relative terms—that there
are varying shades of truth and truth telling, tempered by the
purpose for telling it, and the anticipated result when it is told.
As a result, some leaders shy away from telling their people the
hard truth. Why? I can only guess that some are perhaps concerned that employees can't be trusted with it, or that they will
be upset when confronted with the facts, or maybe even that
they will leak the information to competitors or to the press.

In my experience, this is one of the biggest mistakes a leader can make.

I think that the greatest fear we all have, one everyone has to some degree, is fear of the unknown. When you're home alone at night and you hear an unexplained noise, the natural reaction is to be uneasy until you can determine what the source of the noise was. Similarly, in business, it's human nature for people to have concerns or worries when, for example, your company was just purchased or has merged with a larger competitor. And if the issue is left unexplained, these concerns and worries can become debilitating to people and to the organizations in which they work. In the wake of massive organizational change or disruption, employees wonder about all kinds of possibilities, including, "What's going to happen with my company?" or, "What's going to happen with my job?" or, "What's going to happen with me?"

These kinds of worries are completely rational, and they're often not unfounded. When mobile communications provider T-Mobile USA began to execute its merger with MetroPCS, it announced in April 2013 a series of layoffs that quietly deleted up to four hundred of the company's highest-paid positions from the marketing and operations group of its Seattle-area headquarters. This took place soon after the company laid off more than forty-two hundred call center and other workers earlier in the year.[1] And in March 2013, First California Bank announced that it would lay off fifty-five of its headquarters employees as a direct result of its acquisition by PacWest Bancorp, with other layoffs expected in areas where the two banks have overlapping branches.[2]

Companies going through times of difficulty or change may unintentionally spark fear within their people, creating an environment where employees are worried about their future. Summed up, these examples describe the fear of the unknown. This type of employee concern can wreak havoc. Like a particularly aggressive flu, it can spread quickly—not just within the company but also to suppliers, customers, and others. A leader has the responsibility to the company and employees to eliminate uncertainty as quickly as possible or be ready to deal with the consequences. And these consequences can be costly for the future of the organization. Effective leaders should be on the lookout for signs of fear on the faces of people who feel they may be at risk and immediately take action to do something about it.

WHY I TELL THE TRUTH

If people are fearful of the unknown, their production, their energy, and the company's morale will all plummet. It's a natural consequence of uncertainty in the workplace. That's not good for an organization or for its customers. In the extreme, such fears can lead to anxiety disorders, which, according to Jerilyn Ross, president of the Anxiety Disorders Association of America, "all involve irrational, seemingly uncontrollable and frightening thoughts, which often results in avoidance behavior. And in all cases, the person with the disorder is fully aware that their behavior is irrational. . . What's more, in most cases the disorder impairs the person's normal functioning."[3]

As a leader, what do you do? How do you resolve this uncertainty, and this fear?

Believe it or not, the most effective way to rid an organization of fear of the unknown is simple: tell people the truth. Sounds too easy, doesn't it? Maybe it does, but telling the truth is often easier said than done for many leaders. It's not that they want to lie or tell untruths; it's just that they don't think their people or their organizations or their stakeholders are ready to hear the truth just yet. Indeed, they may be fully committed to telling the truth—when they think the time is right.

I have discovered through my own leadership experiences over the years that people can deal with the truth. Even when it's not good news, when they know what's going on, understand how the situation may affect them, and grasp what they're up against, most will start to adjust and make plans. In other words, the negative energy created by worrying is replaced with positive, productive actions and attitudes.

I always tell our people that they're entitled to get answers to every question they have. I let them know I'm not going to defend myself when it comes to their questions, but I will explain what's going on. I also tell them that while they're entitled to answers to every question, that doesn't mean that they're going to like the answers. But it's going to be truthful, and I know they can deal with the truth. This might create additional questions, but we'll get through them. And we do.

I also don't think it's right for leaders to withhold the truth hoping to get the timing just right or trying to benefit from a big splash with the news. They owe it to their people to get the truth out to them as quickly as possible—and I mean *absolutely* as quickly as they possibly can. You're not going to build trust if you don't do this. You're not going to motivate and inspire people if you don't. You're not going to be an effective leader if you don't. I don't care how bad the news may be, you've got to treat your people like the adults they are and provide them with the information they need to make their own decisions. It sounds simple, but it requires discipline and action.

At Umpqua, we've completed many acquisitions over the years. One of the first steps I take after a transaction is official is to call a town hall meeting where I address everyone in the company we've just acquired. I know that the people in these organizations are anxious and nervous. They have questions about what's going to happen, both to their organization and to them personally. During these meetings, we introduce ourselves, explain the next steps in the integration process, and allow our new associates to get a peek into the Umpqua culture and what it stands for—and what it will mean to them. I also make a point of quickly getting to the question, "What's going to happen to me?" because I realize that until I do, they're not really listening to anything else we have to say. They want—and need—to know the answer to, "What about me?"

I know that there's a chief auditor somewhere in the room thinking, "Ray, your company already has a chief auditor, and I have that position here. You don't need two of us, do you? Am I going to be the one who lands on your layoff list?" At Umpqua, we've taken a clear position with our staff when the issue of layoffs comes up—whether in an acquisition, department consolidation, or simple organizational changes—that we have no plans to eliminate people from the organization. Our approach, which we explain in detail to our new employees, is that, yes, there will be job redundancies resulting in position eliminations. However, those are positions, not people. If it turns out that your job is going to be eliminated, we want you to apply for one of the 150 open positions that we're recruiting for—and hope that among all those vacancies, you'll find something that works for you.

We're truthful with people. We put everything on the table, and we let them deal with the fallout in whatever manner they choose. By being absolutely truthful, you will be helping your people get answers to their questions. As an added benefit you'll also be helping them find their way through these uncertain times.

Communicating early and often, and in as many different ways as possible, is the foundation of my approach to organizational truth telling. I make a point of getting news out to all associates throughout the company on a regular basis. We use many vehicles to accomplish this, including a quarterly broadcast call or video, town halls, focus group meetings, and events centered around the achievements of our associates. We convene town halls for significant milestones like acquisitions, as well as throughout the year within the company's geographic footprint for all Umpqua associates. We use these as an opportunity to communicate with our people as well as to motivate and excite them.

During the worst days of the Great Recession, we increased the number of town halls because we realized how critical it was to ensure that everyone was aware of the actions management was taking to position the company for better days. It was our way of helping to relieve at least some of the anxiety our people felt about the uncertainty of the economic climate at the time. We helped bring some certainty into their lives—the certainty that we were doing everything we possibly could to ensure that their company would remain strong no matter how bad things got.

When we started conducting town halls almost twenty years ago, we set aside time during the meetings to address our associates' questions. Given Umpqua's unique culture, we accomplished this in an unusual yet productive manner. Part of taking away the fear of the unknown is making sure you're listening to and answering your associates' questions, because these are windows into their concerns and perspective. Before our first town hall, we asked our associates to submit their questions to our Culture Department—anonymously, if that was their preference. In other words we were giving them permission to ask any question they wanted to—I mean *any* question.

During our town halls, I answer every associate's questions with this proviso: I must read their questions exactly as they wrote them. The reason for this is I don't want them to think I'm going to water down the sharpness of any question. I'm committed to taking on even the most difficult issues our associates bring forward and addressing them directly and honestly. Over the years, the anonymous question segment of our town halls has grown into an important communication tool, enabling management to get the truth out while answering our associates' concerns.

Why anonymous? You want your people to feel safe that there will not and cannot be retribution against them for asking the kinds of questions that might shine a light on any mistakes or bad decisions. We're human, after all, and not perfect. To require your people to stand up in front of a large group of coworkers with a microphone and ask a tough question—maybe a scary question to them—of the CEO can be nonproductive and a complete morale buster. That's a sure way to kill any sense of honest exchange, and I can guarantee that you aren't going to get many of those tough questions. And don't forget: if you get caught not being truthful or misleading your associates, even in an innocent way, you're digging a hole of distrust that you may never be able to get out of. It takes a long time for people to forget something like that, if they ever truly do.

Our quarterly broadcasts and focus group meetings are used for different purposes, but are just as effective in communicating the truth to our associates. Every quarter, the day after our earnings announcement is made public, I hold a broadcast call or video for our associates and explain the company's financial prospects, as well as any other pertinent news, including recognition of associates who have made a significant contribution in that quarter. At the end of these broadcasts, I always let everyone know that should they have questions to call or e-mail them to me so I can respond.

Yes, that's right. We have more than twenty-five hundred associates at Umpqua, and I answer each of their questions as fast as I can—usually within the same day. It's one of the most effective things I can do as a leader. It clearly demonstrates my commitment to our associates and my respect for their experience and perspective, and it reinforces our culture of telling the truth. I lead by example, and I expect all of our company's other leaders to follow suit. It's the right thing to do, and it helps relieve uncertainty in our organization, along with any fears that our associates might have about the future of the organization and their place in it.

Our focus group meetings are more in-depth. These are called on a moment's notice on an ad hoc basis. I invite ten to twelve of our associates to join me for a cup of coffee to discuss the company. I purposely do not invite management, only staff from all parts of the company. When we meet, I solicit and encourage associates to provide me with honest and constructive criticism of the company. Anything and everything is on the table, from the coffee we supply in our stores to the internal processes we use to train and promote associates. I tell them, "We can't expect our company to get better if we're not aware of what we're doing poorly or inefficiently." After a couple of minutes, I have no problem getting an earful of feedback about improvements we should consider making. I'm personally committed to following through on the feedback I receive during these meetings. The actions taken to correct issues that come up prove to our associates that we care about making things better and that we listen to them. These sessions are particularly invaluable in more difficult times.

Some people think that being truthful is a courageous act, and for some people it may be. However, I personally don't think it's courageous to be truthful; I think it's the right thing to do. If you think about it, telling the truth should be the easiest thing in the world to do—in good times and in bad. And no matter how easy or hard it is, telling the truth is one of the best antidotes you have in your leadership toolbox to combat the uncertainty that can distract your people from doing the work they need to do to the best of their abilities.

If you're not going to be truthful with yourself, your people, and the issues at hand, how do you expect to get better? How do you expect to resolve the issues that every organization and every leader inevitably face?

When I think about leading through uncertainty, the winners in business are the leaders who are truthful with their people when times are challenging and the news isn't good. I think it's tempting for a leader to think, *The news is really bad, and I hate to be the one who has to tell my people that. Maybe we better hold off and not tell them until I can figure out a better time.* This does far more harm than they'll ever dream of. People can deal with the truth. I think in the scheme of things, some people might tell us that a leader can be too direct, or too blunt, and scare the heck out of people. I agree that the way you communicate is very important, but I believe people would rather know the facts than be led down the Yellow Brick Road to some fantasyland that doesn't really exist.

BEING TRUTHFUL WITH YOURSELF

Being truthful with your people requires that you first be truthful with yourself. If you're in the habit of deluding yourself, then this will certainly carry over to the interactions you have with others at work and in your personal life.

UCLA basketball coach John Wooden is considered to be one of the greatest leaders ever. His record with UCLA included four 30–0 seasons, eighty-eight consecutive victories, thirty-eight straight NCAA tournament victories, twenty PAC 10 championships, and ten national championships. According to Wooden, his father was convinced that being honest with yourself and others is the key to living a successful life. He prescribed two "sets of three" to John and his brothers for living their lives. According to Wooden, "Dad's two sets of threes were a compass for me to do the right thing and behave in a proper manner."

The first set of three was focused on being honest with the other people in your life:

Never lie.

Never cheat.

Never steal.

The second set of three was focused on being honest with yourself:

No whining.

No complaining.

No excuses.[4]

But why *not* be truthful with yourself? What's the risk?

Fear of failure is a big one. Some people think to themselves, *What will my peers think of me if I go out on a limb and the limb breaks? What will my family think of me? Let's just ignore the problem and maybe it will go away soon and something good will happen.*

Fear can paralyze you, and it can cause you to avoid the truth. The fear paralysis reflex is a very real thing, and it's part of our genetic wiring from the time we're in the womb. Newborns who perceive a threatening event to be a danger to them are frozen and unable to cope. Physically there's an immediate and real motor paralysis marked by prolonged and generalized immobility, unresponsiveness, and a sudden drop in heart rate.[5] In adults, the fear paralysis reflex is marked by withdrawal, a fear of being placed into different circumstances, and avoidance of anything new and unfamiliar.[6]

Pretend for a moment that you were diagnosed by your doctor with a cancerous tumor that could potentially kill you. Would you tell your loved ones and your work associates the truth—that you were facing a serious health situation—or would you pretend that there was no problem at all? I believe that you ultimately cause more harm, in both your personal and business life, when you deny the truth of the situation to yourself and to others.

Today Odwalla is a healthy beverage and nutrition bar manufacturer known for the playful names of its products, including classics like Strawberry C Monster and Mango Tango fruit smoothies, and Banana Dunk and Choco-Walla bars. Established in 1980, this company based in Half Moon Bay, California, was acquired by Coca-Cola in 2001, with approximately nine hundred employees and annual revenues of about $121 million.[7] Looking at this thriving, profitable company now, it's hard to believe that less than two decades ago, Odwalla was rocked by a tragedy that brought it to the brink of disaster.

In October 1996, sixty-six people became ill after consuming Odwalla's unpasteurized apple-based juice products, which were contaminated with *Escherichia coli* bacteria. Fourteen were children who suffered permanent physical damage, and one was a toddler who died as a result of drinking the tainted juice. Almost overnight, sales dropped 90 percent, and the company's stock plunged 34 percent. Soon Odwalla was facing more than twenty personal injury lawsuits, a grand jury investigation, and $6.5 million in product-recall expenses.[8]

Said company CEO Stephen Williamson at the time, "Our vision statement is about nourishing the body whole, yet people were getting sick from our product. Then a little girl named Anna died from our apple juice, and Odwalla's world changed forever. Our company will never be the same."[9]

What enabled Odwalla to survive such a devastating event?

In a word, *truth*.

Instead of hiding their collective heads in the sand, hoping the situation would blow over or go away, as soon as it was clear that the company's products were the source of the *E. coli* outbreak, the members of Odwalla's leadership team were mobilized to action. Within forty-eight hours, the company removed every single one of its products containing either carrot or apple juice from forty-six hundred retail stores in the United States and Canada. As the crisis ran its course, Odwalla's core leadership team met every fifteen minutes to share the latest news and information and make decisions (as the crisis abated, meeting frequency was reduced to once an hour, then twice a day, and eventually once a day).[10]

Odwalla's leadership team communicated the truth early and often—quickly taking public responsibility for the *E. coli* outbreak and instituting regular company-wide conference calls. The company bought ads in local newspapers where Odwalla sold its products to alert customers to the outbreak, offer to cover the medical expenses of affected consumers, and keep the public up-to-date on recent developments and the company's plans for the future.

By December 1996, just two months after the crisis began, Odwalla introduced a sophisticated quality control system and installed expensive flash-pasteurization machinery to ensure the safety of its products. Today Odwalla's tragedy is a distant memory, and the company has remained back on track.[11]

I believe the reason Odwalla was able to survive its near-death experience was that Williamson and his leadership team refused to compromise when it came to telling the truth—no matter what the cost was to the company. They were honest with themselves and with employees, vendors, customers, and government regulators.

So what can leaders do to encourage their people to be truthful with themselves?

If you're in a management position, that means you've successfully passed some trials and tribulations to get promoted. In my case, people who work for me are well compensated, and with that comes an expectation that they will deal with issues and problems in a truthful and respectful manner. If I were to discover somebody who wasn't doing that, would that make me angry? Most likely, yes, because a fundamental expectation isn't being met, and they're jeopardizing the trust I've worked so hard to build with our people. But the most important thing

I can do is to ask them what they're doing about it and get them to acknowledge the bigger picture.

I've been in situations where I've had to tell people, "Come back tomorrow at 8:00 a.m. with your game plan, and tell me how you're going to dig us out of the problem you created." I'm sure they didn't sleep well that night, but that was the only way that they were going to find a solution. They always do.

In the business world today, I think there's a fine line between being truthful and not doing anything at all. You're not a liar; you're hiding. Your head's in the sand. You're hiding behind a process or whatever cloud you can dream up. I deal with that on a regular basis where people come to me and I'm not happy with what's going on because I don't think they've evaluated the situation thoroughly enough or maybe they're not even aware of it. One of the traits I look for in a leader is for them to have control. That means they know what's going on within their department or division. They're on top of it—they're driving the boat and the boat's not dragging them along into deeper water.

I want my people to be able to say confidently to me, "Yes, we're aware of that problem, and it's a big one. I don't have it figured out yet, but we're working on it. Give me until Wednesday, and I'll come back to you with how we're going to deal with it." That confidence tells me that the person isn't in denial and is aware of the problem, actively trying to understand its scope, and working on a solution. That's positive, that's progress. People do sometimes freeze up because of the size of the problem and their fear of dealing with it. And I think that leaders sometimes have to give their people a nudge to keep them going in the right direction.

FOR REFLECTION

- Shying away from telling your people the hard truth is one of the biggest mistakes a leader can make. Is your instinct to tell the truth, even in difficult times?

- Telling the truth isn't easy for some leaders. How easy or hard is it for you?

- Do you ever withhold telling the truth until you think "the time is right"? Under what circumstances do you do this?

- What are some of the most effective channels you use to communicate with your people, and what could you do to improve them?

- What are you doing to be truthful with your people? Yourself?

3

Problems and the Healing Process

Leadership is solving problems. The day soldiers stop bringing you their problems is the day you have stopped leading them. They have either lost confidence that you can help or concluded that you do not care. Either case is a failure of leadership.
—Colin Powell

Leaders will always be challenged by problems. It's a natural part of their job. Exactly how they tackle the problems they face will determine how others perceive their leadership skills. And whether we like it or not, perception is important. Sometimes it's not what we accomplish that resonates with others; it's what we do and how we act in the heat of battle. This is what builds a leader's reputation, good or bad.

While business problems and challenges don't happen only during difficult or uncertain times, they are more common then—and often worse. It's up to leaders to step up and take visible action when serious issues face their organization. Ignoring them is not an option. And there are benefits to taking action:

organizational healing can begin immediately, and whatever the problems may be, they will be resolved more quickly.

From the beginning of time, leaders have been tested in how they will deal with serious issues facing their company. Others are always watching to see if they will really face up to the difficulties and take action or shrink from their responsibilities and do nothing. It's a test, and some of these tests make leaders stronger; others, handled poorly, can gradually chip away at self-confidence and destroy leadership skills. In many ways, strong leadership is fragile. Although this sounds like an oxymoron, leadership can be diminished by failing to lead, and action can be taken away by failing to act.

One basic fundamental of leadership is the ability to face the problems, difficulties, and issues that every business confronts daily. You can't walk away from problems and truly believe that somehow that issue will magically disappear. It just doesn't happen. And if you think it will, I'm willing to wager that the problem you think went away will be back again, and even stronger.

Too often when people face a problem in their personal or business life, they're tempted to put off taking the very actions that could resolve the problem. They end up dragging it out instead of doing the most expeditious thing: solving it and moving on. When a problem drags out, it can put things at risk in a company or in our personal lives. Ignoring these problems puts relationships at risk as resentments can, and most often do, build up and damage relationships.

For some leaders, delay can seem to be a reasonable strategy for success. If you don't make a decision, then how can you fail? Interestingly enough, the word *decision* has its root in two Latin words: *de* (down from) and *cado* (fall), and the various forms of the combined word (*decido*) can mean anything from "to fall down," "to collapse," "to sink," "to perish," and even "to fall dead." These meanings all point to the dilemma that some leaders find themselves in when making a decision. If they make the *wrong* decision, they may very well go through the organizational equivalent of falling down or falling dead. The solution? Don't make any decisions, or put them off until they're overtaken by events.

At Umpqua we expect people to make decisions. I would rather our associates make an honest mistake that they have the opportunity to learn a lesson from than delay or entirely put off making a decision because they're afraid that they might fail. I don't want our associates to be afraid to make a decision, and I do everything I can to reinforce that in our unique corporate culture.

We also have a standard that we're reminded of frequently at Umpqua Bank, and it's related to solving problems: We should never complain down or sideways in the organization. If our associates face a problem that they can't solve or an issue that's troubling them, we want them to complain "up." The reason is simple: your peers and the people below you likely can't fix your problem. When we *do* complain sideways or down, and we've all done it from time to time, we're reinforcing the old saying that misery loves company. You just made somebody else feel lousy or made them worry. What's the point? That's counterproductive and inconsiderate. You need to complain up to those people who, if you let them know what's going on, are most likely to have the ability to help you fix the issue. It's common sense.

THE STATE OF DENIAL

When uncertainty reigns in the world, when the economy has gone south, when your company is having problems, it's easy to avoid facing the reality of the situation. When the housing market tanked in 2008, a lot of banks faced significant loan losses. Some bankers at the time were saying things like, "Well, I don't think this situation is going to last very long. It's just a small bump in the road and soon we'll be back on track. Let's not worry about it."

As it turned out, these people were figuratively placing their heads in the sand and entering a deep state of denial about the tough problems that existed. They were not preparing for the distinct possibility that the economy could get worse. As we now know, the economy *did* get far worse, eventually triggering the Great Recession that continues to haunt us today. The financial industry suffered greatly during this time, and it has yet to fully recover.

Over the past five years, hundreds of banks have failed, and business in general in the United States was in crisis. The American public also suffered terribly as home foreclosures climbed to all-time highs and the government-reported unemployment rate tied with or exceeded the 10 percent milestone during the last few months of 2009. Many Americans dealt successfully with this economic crisis, and many, due to no fault of their own, ultimately could not survive the storm financially. Others had the resources but failed to use them to position themselves for better days and are now feeling the effects of not taking action. In some ways, they were not being as truthful with themselves as they could have been. By not facing up and dealing with the situation as it truly existed, their problems festered, and, more times than not, they ended up with a more difficult and longer-lasting problem.

Facing up to the reality of your situation, no matter how good or how bad it may be, is the right thing to do. What other choice do you have? How else do you resolve issues and get through tough times if you won't honestly deal with your issues? There are many positive attributes that can result from people facing the truth. Others have respect for the person who is willing to do the right things in tough times. People are naturally resilient, and they will give the benefit of the doubt to others if they believe that actions are being taken to improve the issue. They will understand. Communicating often with your people and telling them the truth is one of the best ways to gain their respect and admiration.

In early 2007, Umpqua Bank was the largest independent community bank in Northern California. When the first cracks in the housing market were starting to appear, I clearly remember driving north out of Sacramento, California, which was to become the epicenter of the housing crash in the state. As I drove north on the interstate, I remember looking out the window and seeing hundreds, if not thousands, of brand-new roofs on each side of the highway. There were no trees, just new homes going up at an incredibly fast rate. Acre after acre of former pastureland was being converted into neighborhoods. It didn't take a rocket scientist to see a potential problem.

I remember wondering as I drove through this massive construction project, *How can the Sacramento infrastructure sustain this type of growth without experiencing difficulties?* (It couldn't.) Even scarier was the thought, *What would be the impact to housing here if supply and demand for housing was to become seriously unbalanced?* (It would not be good.) I suspected that the impact could be devastating for home owners and home builders alike, along with the banks that were serving as their lenders.

When I got back to my office in Portland, Oregon, I asked my lending executives to brief me on the company's total exposure in the real estate market throughout our geographic footprint. I was most interested in loans for home construction and loans associated with developing neighborhoods from raw land. The report I received was not encouraging. At the time, Umpqua had more than $700 million of loans within these broad categories. We had a problem.

Now that we had identified the problem, the question was what we were going to do about it. We had two main choices. One, we could hunker down and do nothing, hoping the housing market wouldn't contract further. This was certainly a possible—and attractive—outcome, but there was no indication at the time that the economy was suddenly going to get better. Or, two, we could deal with the situation as honestly and as transparently as we possibly could. If all this economic roiling continued, we needed to take action to protect our company from this potentially dangerous financial exposure.

We took the latter course of action.

Shortly after identifying the risk to Umpqua if the market got worse, we made the decision to go public with the possibilities. During an investor conference in New York, I informed investors what Umpqua's exposure was in this market and let them know that at that time, the loans in question were in good shape. However, I also let them know that should the housing market worsen and should home prices fall significantly, making it difficult to sell homes, then these loans could be at risk.

Investor response to these statements at the time wasn't positive. Our stock price was clobbered, and it's safe to say that at that moment, Wall Street did not think highly of us. However, as I look back at that decision to put our issue of potential loan losses on the table for all to see, I believe it was one of the best business decisions I have ever made. Why? Because once the problem was exposed, we had to deal with it. That meant that the healing process could begin.

Over the next few years, we did just that. And because of our quick action, Umpqua Bank came through the Great Recession with a stronger balance sheet than when we entered it. Yes, we suffered losses, as did many other financial institutions, but we also navigated the company through the crisis faster than most of our peers and gained respect from both Wall Street and Main Street by being honest and transparent with our financials during a time when banks were viewed by many as the Evil Empire, and too many tried to ignore their own troubled loans.

Avoiding the state of denial is not difficult, but it does take no small amount of fortitude. Accept the facts, try to corral the potential damages, and then get busy doing what you know you are supposed to do. Acknowledging the problem is probably 50 percent of the resolution process, since once you've acknowledged the problem, you have to act on it. There are many examples where people have demonstrated their willingness to accept responsibility and then do something about it.

Consider Jamie Dimon, CEO and chairman of JPMorgan Chase. He was in charge when his company experienced a multibillion-dollar trading loss. Dimon, one of the most respected bank executives in the world, is deservedly well known and well regarded for his leadership skills. Once this crisis was identified by people within JPMorgan Chase, Jamie was quick to acknowledge it. He didn't try to make it appear anything other than what it was—in his own words, "a terrible, egregious mistake." He clearly indicated that this issue was the result of "flawed, complex, poorly reviewed, poorly executed, and poorly monitored" activities within JPMorgan Chase.[1]

Yes, the problem created a black eye for his firm, and it created more issues for the financial industry as a whole once Congress got involved. But he stood up and took responsibility for the mess. If he hadn't taken this approach and hadn't done the right thing, that crisis could have been an ongoing problem for JPMorgan Chase as I write this today.

There are numerous examples where problems were ignored or deliberately hidden, prolonging the pain and keeping the individuals and organizations in the glare of the spotlight for longer than if they had just faced their problems and addressed them as they arose.

Consider the sorry saga of Lance Armstrong. The authorities caught some members of his cycling team taking performance-enhancing drugs during the Tour de France. After dragging the sport through the mud, some of Armstrong's teammates admitted to the doping and suffered the consequences. But here's the question: Can you think of their names? I bet you can't.

These guys confessed to their cheating, paid the price, and the problem quickly disappeared from the public eye for these individuals. But Lance Armstrong chose to deny any involvement in the doping scandal and refused to admit that he participated even when teammates reported differently. He attacked those who reported that he'd taken illegal drugs, beating them down in the press and even taking some to court. What he did was perpetuate the problem, ruin his reputation, and give the sport a black eye that will likely take many years for it to recover from. If he had confessed by saying "Yes, I also took the same drugs," when this was becoming an issue ten years ago, I'm convinced it wouldn't be in the news today. Sure, it would have been bad for Lance and the sport for a while, but it would have disappeared more quickly.

TIMING IS EVERYTHING

Timing is important, but I would caution leaders in any business or industry that you're better off admitting to and dealing with problems earlier rather than later. That said, I don't think anybody should be in a rush to say, "Oh, let me tell you all my problems," when five minutes later those problems get resolved. There are issues that come up that you can resolve yourself, and there's no need to go out and tell the world about it. But if it's something that's going to have a significant impact on your business or personal life, it's not going to get fixed until you start addressing it. By taking action, it's like going public with yourself so the healing process can begin. The most important thing is not to deny the existence of problems when they are at hand.

What would you do if you were getting ready to go on vacation, and your roof had a small leak? Would you ignore it and say, "I'll get it fixed when we get back," or would you address the problem and get the leak fixed immediately? If you ignored the problem, it's quite possible that when you returned from your vacation, the water damage to your home while you were gone could be significant. What might have been a quick one- or two-hour fix when you discovered the problem has now turned into a five-week-long redo of the entire top floor of your house because you denied that there was a problem that needed to be addressed.

I believe that like those leaders who drag out or avoid making decisions, there can be an element of fear of failure and financial harm that sometimes prevents people from dealing with the problems in their organizations. Fear of failure can cloud a person's perspective on what is right or wrong and what is critical to a company's future. While the ineffective leader will remain stuck—paralyzed in a state of inaction by this fear of failure—the strong leader can shake this off and get back on the healing road by addressing the problem.

Another point of view is that people wait too long to address issues, and when they wait too long, it's normally too late to recover. So as soon as you see a problem that needs to be addressed with your people, you'll know if there's a timing issue and when the right time is to deal with the problem. Deciding when to let people know what's going on needs to be thought through intelligently with management. Just keep in mind that the longer you wait, the longer the fear of the unknown continues to grow and can create a more significant problem.

ENCOURAGE YOUR PEOPLE TO STEP UP

People have a tremendous amount of respect for individuals who are brave enough to stand up and face the music. I'm not talking about people who face the music after ten years of denying it (see my comments on Lance Armstrong above), but people who face the music when the problem first occurs. That's a big deal.

We're all afraid of our own personal failures, of losing face, losing our jobs, and of the hit to our egos for having a problem or making a mistake. But in my experience, most observers aren't focused on that: they just want to know what you're doing to fix the problems you face. If people would simply focus on saying, "Look, this is the problem, and yes it's unfortunate we have to deal with it, but the fact is that it happened, there's nothing anybody can do about it, so let's move on and solve it," their organizations would benefit greatly. Instead of worrying about how it will look to others that they made a mistake, what everyone in your organization should be interested in now is asking, "What the hell are we doing to solve this problem, and how quickly can we get this straightened out?"

Like all other businesses, Umpqua Bank has gone through significant uncertainty and difficulties from time to time. When the recession hit and uncertainty was the topic of the day, we made many decisions to help navigate the company to a better place. In late 2007, we decided to delay all salary increases for six months for those making over a certain wage level, including me and everyone else on the management team. This was going to be a tough pill to swallow for some of my people; however, to me, it felt like the right thing to do. I wanted my associates to understand that we all might be asked to make sacrifices to get through this mess together. Some of our executives felt this decision was too extreme and not needed at the time, that things weren't bad enough yet. They worried about the impact this decision would have on morale and our associates' reaction.

I disagreed. I felt that taking action ahead of the growing problem was the right step to take. However, I did believe that the communication of my decision could not be delegated to others. I had to handle it: my people needed to hear from me. I needed to face the music and put a face on the decision we had made.

In a live call to our associates, I shared with them what I had decided. I went through in great detail why it was necessary to delay salary increases and explained the implications to everyone. I also made myself available after that call to answer any questions or concerns they might have had after thinking about my decision. I was confident that our associates would give me the benefit of the doubt even while making a decision that had a negative impact on their pocketbooks.

Even I was surprised by the reaction from our people. After the call was over, I received more than a hundred e-mails from associates throughout the company letting me know they understood. One comment was, "It's great to see you're doing the right thing for our company," and another simply said, "Thank you." It was truly heartwarming. Dealing with problems in an organization isn't always a pleasant thing to do, but it's always the right thing to do.

FOR REFLECTION

- Every organization has problems. Identify major problems your organization is facing.

- Do you relish making decisions, or do you avoid them? How does the approach you pursue affect your ability to solve your organization's problems?

- Do you routinely face up to the reality of your situation, or do you tend to hide your head in the sand? What is the impact of the approach you pursue on your ability to solve your organization's problems?

- What do you do to encourage your people to step up and deal with problems?

4

Control and Uncertainty

I do not want to foresee the future. I am concerned with taking care of the present. God has given me no control over the moment following.
—Mahatma Gandhi

Leaders often face a dilemma: How can they be responsible for things that are beyond their direct control and outcomes that may not be entirely predictable in uncertain times? The simple truth is that they can't. But despite that fact, many leaders feel responsible anyway and make every effort to control the uncontrollable and try to create certainty out of uncertain situations. I believe this is a mistake. As leaders, we must first take responsibility for those areas we can control and then prepare for uncertainty while recognizing its inherent unpredictability.

Risk and uncertainty are natural parts of any business. However, leaders should focus time, resources, and attention on the things that they can affect and control, not the things they can't. While you must be prepared for the uncertainties you can't control—with a plan in place if they come to pass—you can't dwell on them. Put the bulk of your energy into the things you can control and leverage for the benefit of your business.

Some of you may wonder, "What's the big deal here? As leaders, of course we should control our areas of responsibility and be prepared for surprises." I agree that even in the best of times, these are basic tenets of a good leader. However, there are different aspects of control and uncertainty that may catch you off-guard when times become more difficult and you find yourself in the fog of rapid change in your markets. It's important to understand the human element associated with each of these factors and how they can affect your business.

MANAGING THE RISK ELEMENT

In any business, one of the most important areas of concern is risk. In fact, many large businesses have entire departments dedicated to risk management. Risk comes in many different forms, some small and others significant to the future of a business. One thing is certain: it all must be managed. Otherwise you could be building a foundation for trouble that will haunt you in future years.

Let's again consider the example of Umpqua Bank. As a financial institution, our primary function is to manage risk. It's what banks do day in and day out, and our risks come from almost every area of our business. For example, we loan money, obviously a risky business. We try to mitigate that risk by requiring loan applicants to provide us with information about their creditworthiness and ability to pay back the loan.

We also build loan portfolios where concentrations in a particular class of loan could place the company at more risk then we should tolerate.

Think back to 2008 when the housing bubble truly popped. If a bank had too much of its total loan portfolio in residential or home construction, it faced serious issues as the borrowers defaulted and the loans quickly went bad. Some banks managed this risk element poorly and subsequently failed. They thought that this area of originating loans was profitable (and it most definitely was before the housing bubble burst) and that the housing market would *never* crash (it had been on a steep upward swing for a number of years after all), so why wouldn't they continue to make these types of loans? As we learned, history is not a reliable predictor of the future.

In addition, many of these banks got caught up in the euphoria of the times and failed to prepare for the uncertain possibility that the real estate market could very well take a dive. Some stuck their heads in the sand and embraced denial. Many of these banks now no longer exist. Consider Lehman Brothers, which in 2007 had peak revenues of $59 billion and in 2008 ranked number thirty-seven in the Fortune 500 before it went bankrupt that same year. What happened to this venerable Wall Street investment bank, founded in 1850? During the height of the housing bubble that peaked in 2007, Lehman Brothers borrowed heavily to purchase subprime mortgage-backed securities and real estate, eventually reaching a leverage ratio of at minimum 31:1. That is, for every dollar in equity that Lehman brothers owned by way of these securities, the company was in debt to the tune of thirty-one dollars. (A federal bankruptcy court-sponsored report later put this ratio at closer to 44:1[1].)

This house of cards came crashing down when the housing bubble burst and Lehman Brothers' losses quickly grew and became unsustainable. The company announced that it would seek Chapter 11 bankruptcy protection on September 15, 2008.[2] Lehman Brothers was eventually liquidated, with its various businesses sold off to a variety of different financial services firms.

However, many other institutions did a great job of managing the risk in their loan portfolios, faced the music on losses, ensured they were capital healthy, and came through this difficult period stronger than when they entered it. They are now the winners.

Every kind of business has similar issues as it relates to managing risk. Think about the retail store manager who's responsible for preparing orders for the Christmas holidays. His job (among many others, to be certain) is to make sure the store has enough of the right kind of inventory on hand to meet customers' shopping needs. Ordering too little or too much can have profoundly negative consequences on the business's cash flow, sales revenues, staffing, reputation, and much more. The permanency of this manager's job may very well depend on how accurate he is in making his forecasts of consumer behavior.

The moral of the story is that every company has risk that the management teams of all companies have to manage every day.

WORRY ABOUT WHAT YOU CAN CONTROL

As the CEO of my company, I expect my direct reports to stay on top of all the issues, goals, and opportunities that they have control over. I often tell my associates that it's appropriate to worry about those things that they can change and control. I believe this is that the issues they face should be well in hand and controllable while they steer their divisions to meet goals, resolve problems, or take advantage of opportunities. I also let them know that it's not productive for them to worry about those things over which they have no control. For the most part, uncertainty is uncontrollable; however, you can and should be prepared for any number of possible outcomes.

Business owners or executives who have goals they're expected to achieve are going to move heaven and earth to be successful and produce results. However, worrying about uncertain events that may or may not occur can bog them down and cause them to second-guess, hesitate, or wait before acting. Acts of God like floods, earthquakes, and getting hit by a meteorite are clearly obvious uncertainties that could conceivably happen and harm the status of your business.

To me it's detrimental to worry about these possibilities. And yet in the same breath, I will tell you that you should do your best to prepare for them. Do you have the right insurance? Can you back up your computer system quickly? Do you have a disaster recovery plan in place that all employees are aware of and knowledgeable about? So I think you worry about the things you can control and prepare for the things that you don't have control over or have uncertainty about.

The overriding idea is that I'm going to be very focused on those things that I can affect. I will always have specific answers to what we're going to do to achieve our goals. However, I'm not going to worry about what happens if an earthquake rocks Portland and blows the hell out of everything! While we need to be prepared for that (we are, after all, located less than fifty miles to the west of Mount Hood, an

11,240-foot-tall volcano that's one of the most recently active in the Cascade Volcanic Arc, where the Juan de Fuca plate subducts under the North American tectonic plate, creating volcanic activity in the area), I can't worry about it because it could happen at any time.[3] But we do need to prepare for such an event and be ready for it.

There are other kinds of uncertainties that we also need to anticipate and prepare for. I wonder how many business owners have seen a big-box competitor indicate it's making plans to open a new superstore across the street from them, and wonder, *Now what do we do?*

Why haven't they thought about this possibility before, and why aren't they already prepared to minimize damage to their business in the best way they can? Being proactive with uncertainties is a good exercise, and I highly recommend it. I realize it's impossible to prepare for every possible unknown, but you should prepare for at least the five or six things that could have the greatest impact on your business.

At Umpqua we're large enough to have an enterprise risk department within our company that constantly keeps me and others advised of the level of risk that we have in the different areas of our business. They produce a document every month that details the likelihood of a risk occurring and the impact it would have on our business. We also have ways to measure the level of risk to determine if the risk identified is within our area of comfort. If it is trending into the danger zone, we are warned so we can take whatever action is necessary to prevent, minimize, or correct the deficiency.

Few small businesses, however, have enterprise risk management departments that can keep them out of trouble in the same way ours does. The enterprise risk manager in these companies is instead going to be the business owner or one of its executives or managers. These leaders should anticipate and be prepared for a variety of challenging situations in their businesses and their communities, industries, and markets. And there are people who can help prepare for these uncertainties— from insurance companies, to Certified Public Accountants, to attorneys, and many others. There are plenty of resources that they can use to make sure that they've got the big risks pretty well nailed down. One great resource for small business is to develop an advisory board of directors. Recruit four to six professionals who agree to meet quarterly to discuss your business and your market to help you stay in touch with the competitive landscape and get objective and honest advice about your company and its prospects going forward.

TWO ASPECTS OF A LEADER'S JOB: CONTROLLABLE RESULTS AND UNCERTAINTY

In business, I believe we all understand that we will be held accountable for achieving our goals. It makes little difference if you're part of a large organization or a sole proprietor. We all still have accountability to someone.

When I interview people to join our company in a leadership role, I always try to ascertain whether this person can take control of this department or division, motivate and inspire his or her people, and communicate effectively on progress made before I make the hiring decision. This is also the case with people who currently work for and with me. I am constantly observing and reevaluating their ability to stay in control of their areas of responsibility.

I also believe in giving people the benefit of the doubt. If they have personal confidence in their ability and the respect of their people, and if I know firsthand that they have worked diligently toward achieving their goals, I support them 100 percent, without question. The leader who's making daily progress toward achieving his or her controllable goals will usually be able to anticipate the uncertainties that could derail his or her best efforts and intentions.

One more comment on uncertainties. Most of the time when we think of something happening that would be out of our control, we tend to think of it as having a negative impact on our company or goals. Again, this goes back to our programming. In reality, some uncertainties can be positive and fulfilling. How about the woman who won the lottery? That would be fulfilling and certainly unexpected. In business it could be something as simple as a large sales order coming in unexpectedly or a technological advance in another industry that sparks a new idea and opportunity for your company.

Yes, there's no doubt that many uncertainties can bring challenges for your business, but let's not forget that there are plenty of other unexpected events that provide wind for our sails. We should always try to be prepared for and ready to leverage these as well.

BLACK AND WHITE: MAKING DECISIONS EASY

For the most part, the decisions leaders encounter in business are black or white; in other words, the answer is clear: make it and move on. Should we hire more associates to staff a store that has recently had several retirements? Yes, because if we don't, we won't be able to maintain a stable work schedule, which would potentially have a negative impact on the satisfaction of both our customers and our remaining associates. Should we invest more money in television advertising? No, at least not until someone can show us a direct correlation between running a television ad and an increase in new accounts in the target market.

I believe that making decisions like these is for the most part easy and a matter of course for most leaders. What's difficult is getting the correct information and intelligence so you can make a rational and well-informed decision. I also believe that if you're not careful, the law of diminishing returns can set in during the course of the decision-making process. Some people want to have an extremely high probability of success before they decide to act—well over 50 percent. So they wait. And they wait. And then they wait some more. Most of the time, the new information they receive while they're waiting adds nothing to their final decision. Yes, I realize that there are exceptions to this general statement, but in my experience it's not very often.

For some reason, most people seem to be conditioned to believe that fifty-fifty odds are not very good. In reality, I think fifty-fifty odds are *great*. If you were a baseball player batting .500, that is, you got on first base one out of every two times you were at bat, you'd be a hero. As a leader, you have to recalibrate your expectations.

An executive might tell me, "Ray, we have better than a fifty-fifty chance of success if we decide now. However, if we wait two more weeks and get this done when things are a little bit more in our favor, I'll feel more confident in our success." When that happens, I'll look at this person and say, "Are you kidding me? Your chances are that good? What are you waiting for?" Better than fifty-fifty odds are great, depending on the decision, of course. I say this because as a leader, I have confidence in this person's ability to add another 10 or 15 percent in his or her favor just by getting involved. So get all the critical information you can, but be aware that it's too easy to get bogged down in minutiae and information overload in making decisions. Timely decision making is critical to making progress in the areas you control.

There's another color that can insert itself every so often in the decision-making process: gray. Depending on the complexity of your business or how high you are in the food chain, more decisions can turn gray instead of a simple black or white. These are the decisions that need to be made that don't have a clear answer, or there's more at risk that the decision maker needs to think about before taking the next steps. The gray decisions are the ones that confound decision makers the most. Too often, we stew and worry so much about making the correct decision that we paralyze ourselves and our company.

When I see this happening with the people who report to me, I'll say, "Why are you torturing yourself over this? Why don't you just decide? You're going to feel great about it once it's over and you move on." Of course, it's easier said than done, but some people like to tie themselves up in knots unnecessarily to get to a decision they knew they were going to make anyway. Why get all worked up over this?

Common sense says that you're going to look at the data. You're going to ask people to share information, perspectives, and recommendations with you. You're going to evaluate your own intuition about what you think of these inputs from your people (more on intuition in Chapter 5). What about the person who is in front of you and asking for your decision? What confidence level does he have? People who have confidence in their own skills and abilities and can communicate that to their leader make that leader's job a lot easier when it comes to making decisions that aren't always black and white.

DO YOUR BEST, GET INPUT, AND REMEMBER—IT'S JUST A NUMBER!

At Umpqua Bank, one of our goals is to grow. This means that we want to see our people making progress toward their goals every day. But sometimes people working for me worry too much that their growth number for a particular period will fall short despite their best efforts.

I do like the fact that they're concerned about missing their goals and I like it that they hate to lose, a trait I love in a leader. The people who work directly for me put enough pressure on themselves that it's impossible for me to add any more (well, maybe sometimes). As I said, I *like* working with and dealing with people who want to win.

But at the same time I think most leaders would say that it's the top executive's or business owner's job to make sure an organization's people keep things in perspective. If an associate who has worked hard and in whom you have full confidence falls short on growth goals for the period, that shouldn't be the end of the world. I want my top executives to work hard and meet or exceed expectations. However, from time to time I also tell them (without letting them off the hook) that putting too much pressure on themselves can be dangerous to them and to others. I'll say, "Let's keep this in perspective—and remember it's just a number."

Years ago, Jean-François Manzoni and Jean-Louis Barsoux described something they called the "set-up-to-fail syndrome." According to the authors, when employees fail, their bosses rarely blame themselves for this failure. Perhaps the employee who failed isn't very smart, or maybe isn't motivated to succeed, or can't set priorities, or just doesn't "get it." And while Manzoni and Barsoux concede that there are indeed situations when the reason for failure can be laid squarely at the feet of the employee, in the majority of cases, "an employee's poor performance can be blamed largely on his boss."[4] The manager behavior that leads to this outcome may be accidental, and it may occur with the best intentions, but the results are the same nonetheless: an employee who's been set up by his or her boss to fail.

The mechanism of Manzoni and Barsoux's syndrome works roughly like this. The employee misses a goal, and the boss starts worrying that the employee may not be up to the task. As a result of this worry, the boss focuses more attention on the errant employee, beginning a cycle of micromanagement intended to boost the employee's performance. Instead, the employee interprets this added attention on the part of the boss as a loss of trust and confidence in the employee's capabilities, which causes the employee to withdraw. The more the employee withdraws, the greater attention the boss devotes to the employee, increasing the employee's perception that he or she is not trusted to do a good job. The eventual result is an employee who's paralyzed into a state of inaction, afraid to do anything that might attract further attention from the boss. In the worst case, the employee may quit or be fired.

A good leader knows when to take pressure off their team. If you push too hard for too long, you can create serious morale problems in your organization and burn out your team members, with the result that you could lose good people. You need to know when to push, but you also need to know when to loosen up a little bit. If you've set a deadline of two weeks to get a report done and your employee tells you it's going to be a week late—and I know that she's working hard on it—I'll say, "I know if you jam this out in the next week, the risk of failure goes up a lot. I want you to take your time and do it right. If it's going to be a week late, no, I don't like it, but I'm giving you the extra week to get it done because I want success. I don't want failure."

I can deal with timing. If someone is dragging their feet, that's one thing, but around my company they can't slow down because the velocity of our company (if there were such a thing) would expose them. This goes back to the numbers, the goals, and anxiety. Anxiety is highly contagious in an organization because when you're anxious, you're irritable, testy, and on edge, and you're at risk of making decisions that you might regret later. People need to know they have time to perform and make decisions confidently, and leaders need to give their people the space to succeed without constantly looking over their shoulders and worrying about whether their boss is keeping a close eye on them.

Worry only about those things you can control while preparing for uncertainty—*always*. For those areas you can control, make sure you're giving your people the latitude to make timely and informed decisions advancing you toward your goals. People also need to be reminded every so often that with empowerment comes accountability.

FOR REFLECTION

- What are the greatest risks to your business, and what are you doing to address them?

- What are the major things you can control in your business, and what are the major things that are out of your hands? How are you addressing each?

- How does your organization deal with uncertainty? How do you personally deal with it?

- What is your personal decision-making process, and how can you improve it?

- Do you set up your people to fail? If so, what can you do to change this?

5

Exercise Your Intuition

Intuition will tell the thinking mind where to look next.
—Jonas Salk

Intuition is often associated with expressions like "good guess," "go with your instincts," and "watch for signals," to name a few. I suppose this is because the definition of *intuition* is "to acquire knowledge without inference or rational thought"—in other words, to think without thinking. Some people shy away from their intuition, a big mistake in any organization. Intuition isn't magic, and it's not irrational. Intuition is a powerful, heightened state of awareness that can enable employees to discover opportunities to exceed their customers' expectations—creating experiences that won't soon be forgotten. It's up to leaders to make it safe for their people to exercise and apply their intuition.

While some leaders believe that intuition has no place in business, instead preferring that all decisions of any consequence be based solely on objective data and numbers, I fundamentally disagree with this point of view. Yes, objective data and numbers have their place and must be considered when making decisions, especially those that have the greatest impact on an organization, but intuition also has an important place: it can be powerfully accurate and should not be ignored.

This chapter explores intuition from a different point of view: how employees who are empowered to use their intuition in business settings can make a difference in the prospects of the company. Practiced and used properly, the application of intuition by your people can have strong, positive effects on your company's reputation, brand, and ability to attract customers in good and, even more important, in difficult and uncertain times.

INTUITION AND CUSTOMER RELATIONS

The secret of making intuition work in a business environment is allowing your people to practice and use it. It's as simple as that. I think of intuition as having the skill and ability to listen to clients or customers and then take actions that will surprise and delight them. When you think of intuition in this manner, there is little to no downside. You have nothing to lose and everything to gain in allowing your employees to use their intuition for the good of your company.

Recent studies have shown that trusting your gut can be a powerfully effective approach to decision making. According to a study reported in the November 2012 issue of the journal *Organizational Behavior and Human Decision Processes* by researchers from Rice University, Boston College, and George Mason University, there are specific conditions under which intuition is a good way to make the right decision. Says study coauthor Michael Pratt, "What we found demystifies a lot of the information out there that says that intuition isn't as effective as if you sat down and walked through an analytical approach."[1]

According to the researchers, intuition is most effective when you already have expertise in the area or organization in which you're making your decisions. The more expert you are, the better your intuitive decisions. However, says Erik Dane, the lead author of the study, "Even if you're an expert, intuitive decision-making is better for some types of tasks than others. Tasks that can be solved through predetermined steps, like math problems, are not as conducive to intuitive decision-making as less-structured tasks, which may include certain strategic or human resource management problems."[2]

At Umpqua we seek out associates who are intuitive. These are people who listen well, meaning they are looking for opportunities to exceed customers' expectations, thereby creating an experience that won't soon be forgotten. They are people who will help your company stand out.

I'll never forget the time I spent the night at a Ritz-Carlton Hotel in New York City before leaving the next day for a vacation in Morocco. After my wife and I checked in at the reception desk, a young woman escorted us to our room, and while on the elevator she casually asked about our plans in New York. We explained that this was a brief stopover as we were leaving for Morocco the next morning. She exclaimed, "Really! The head of housekeeping here at the hotel is originally from Morocco and she's always talking about how beautiful it is."

We didn't think too much of the conversation because we needed to get cleaned up before heading out for dinner that evening. When we returned to our room later that night, we were in for a surprise. On our desk was a beautiful coffee table picture book of Morocco, with a note from the head housekeeper telling us her name, where in Morocco she came from, and how much she hoped we would enjoy her wonderful country.

Now, would that have surprised you? Did she make us feel incredibly special? You bet she did. It sounds easy, but actually there were a lot of moving parts to accomplish this small random act of kindness. First, the receptionist must have thought, *Wow, this is a great opportunity to show our guests how customer-friendly our hotel is*. Next, she contacted the head housekeeper, who then took time out of her busy schedule to make arrangements for the book to be purchased at a local bookstore and delivered to our room along with her personal note.

These were people who were empowered by Ritz-Carlton's management to act. Did it make my stay in New York a little more special? Definitely. As you can see, I'm still talking about it. And when I'm in New York, the Ritz is where I stay.

Some people would say, "Wow, what a great thing for that associate to do," and I would agree. But I also recognize, "What a terrific management team." They're allowing their people to exercise and practice their intuition by listening to and looking for opportunities to wow their customers.

Companies like Ritz that empower and incent their people to use their intuition are practicing a form of differentiation. All companies big or small, private or public, are looking for ways to differentiate themselves from their competitors and opportunities to stand out in a positive manner, trying to per-suade potential customers to skip by their competitors and shop with them. It's a basic business survival strategy. Sure—we use marketing, advertising, product delivery systems, the Internet, promotions, and much more to advance our company's name and products, and all of these different things certainly help. But think what happens when you add to the mix empowered people who are encouraged to look for ways to delight their customers. It's transformational, it's a momentum builder, and it's powerful.

LISTEN AND ACT

Too few companies empower and incent their people to use their intuition because too few companies, and therefore too few people, get the opportunity to activate this side of themselves. There are companies that don't practice it at all and companies that are very good at it. In my mind, the companies that excel at it stand out from the rest of the pack, especially when it comes to their customer relations. You need to have great customer relations in both good and bad times.

Intuition is hard to teach, but it can be learned if people are given permission to practice using it without intimidation. The use of this type of intuition can catch on with your people; I like to think of it as being contagious in a good way. Unfortunately many people aren't given the opportunity to practice or use their intuition due to policies and strict procedures handed down by higher-ups. This is a mistake.

When we introduced the idea of empowerment to our associates at Umpqua Bank, we weren't surprised by the deer-in-the-headlights look we received from many of them. At first they were intimidated by the idea of being able to make customer service decisions. We expected this: When a switch has been turned off for a long time, simply turning it back on doesn't produce instant results. We realized we were going to have to make sure our associates understood that it was okay to practice using their new authority.

It turned out, however, that encouraging them wasn't enough to get this engine started. It was very much like the old Life cereal television commercial that aired back in the 1980s with the young brothers who say, "Let's get Mikey! Let's see if he likes it [the cereal]!" In other words, our people wanted assurances from us that it was in fact safe to practice their empowerment and use their intuition. Once we realized what the hesitation was about, we went to work. We introduced new incentive plans that rewarded our people with cash and prizes if they practiced their intuition, and we started an internal recognition plan for those who did. Not only did it start the intuition engine, it created a new level of excitement and enthusiasm within the company that we'd never seen before. Our people were having fun. And our customers benefited from all this practice.

Business leaders have to acknowledge that empowered people can create momentum for an organization with little downside. In good times it's terrific, and in uncertain times, it's incredibly important. Empower your people to practice doing what they think is right for your customers and give them the freedom to enjoy it.

When I write about empowerment, it reminds me that it's about giving our associates here at Umpqua the ability to use their good judgment with our customers. It's liberating: When they have the authority to make customer service decisions, they understand that management trusts them. It also clearly indicates that we believe their opinions and actions count.

In *Leading for Growth*, I wrote about a concept I call *positive passion*, which I described as "optimism coupled with passion." All leaders have to be optimistic and passionate about their goals, actions, and people if they are to be effective. Practicing these two words is not an option for leadership; it's required. I also believe we should add another word to the list, *intuition*. Knowing when and how to use intuition is a competitive edge builder for leaders that shouldn't be ignored. But you have to practice.

At Umpqua, we empower our people so consistently that if they want to do something nice for a customer, they just do it. They don't ask for permission. We trust them—we know they're going to do the right thing. And they do. All twenty-five hundred of them.

KNOW WHEN TO ACT

I believe that using your intuition is related to using your instincts—the two are very closely connected. The worn-out expression that our grandmothers used to tell us that "if it feels too good to be true it probably is" still applies to our personal and business lives. Instincts often warn us that something may be wrong, just as it can alert us when something feels right.

When you walk down a dark alley and hear footsteps behind you, the hair on the back of your neck stands up, and you may think, *I've got to get out of here now!* Your intuition and instincts are telling you that something doesn't feel right, and your brain tells you that you need to act.

This kind of intuition also works in the business environment. For example, you may see a trend in your business or industry that feels wrong or off-base and is worrisome. In cases like this, some people may tell you, "No worries, this is under control, we've got it," and yet you decide, "No, I've got to do something about it," whether that means curtailing operations in one area or providing additional resources in another. The difference between being right or wrong can decide success and failure, business survival and extinction. "Practice makes perfect," as they say, but knowing when to act is when you "put the pedal to the metal!"

So how do you know if you're using your intuition at work, or if you've instead put it on the back burner or hidden it away in a closet? Here's a set of questions you can ask yourself, developed by management professor Eugene Sadler-Smith and organizational development expert Erelly Shefy:

- Do you *trust* your hunches when confronted by an important decision?

- Do you *feel in your body* if a decision is right or wrong?

- Do you put a lot of *faith* in your initial feelings about people and situations?

- Do you put more emphasis on *feelings* than data when you make a decision?

- Do you rely on your *gut feelings* when dealing with people?

- Do you trust your *experience* when arriving at the reasons for making a decision even if you can't explain why?

- Does your intuition often turn out to have been *right* all along?

- What is (or would be) the reaction in your organization to decisions made on the basis that they *felt* right?

- Do you keep your intuitions *close to your chest*? If so, *why*?[3]

All business leaders spend a lot of time on the tangible aspects of their business—the financial reports, the new product launches, the marketing plans, the employee rewards and recognition programs, and much more. They have to pay attention to the tangible aspects of their business, and they should. Unfortunately many don't give enough attention to the intangible elements of their business, which prove in many cases to be what really makes the organization stand apart from competitors. It's also true that when difficulties arise, the intangibles are too often sacrificed or cut out first.

During the Great Recession, I watched companies terminate sustainability programs, slash employee authority, and waive personal and corporate standards—all in the name of cutting costs. I agree that drastic measures are sometimes required. However, management should also weigh the impact these types of actions have on their employees and the messages that they send. I believe leaders need to pay more attention to those intangibles that help form the very foundation of their company. Allowing proper space and time for the use of intuition is certainly one those, as are reputation, culture, ethics, and morals. These are the invisible assets that all great companies possess and are vital to the business and its people.

WHEN YOU TRUST YOUR INTUITION, OPPORTUNITIES FOLLOW

While it's important for leaders to follow their intuition in all business conditions, intuition becomes even more important when conditions are uncertain. When your company's ability to thrive or even survive is in question, you need every good idea you can possibly get, no matter how large or how small it might be.

In a way, acting on your intuition is closely related to being creative. If you're totally analytical and numbers driven, you may end up constraining your thinking within the box the data lays out. When you act on your intuition, you open up your mind to the vast universe of possibilities—many of which may not be the direct result of whatever data your organization is providing you with.

At its core intuition is about listening; it's not some magical thing that you either have or don't have. It's being focused and zeroing in on people. When you're intuitive, you're listening closely to what others have to say, and watching and feeling intently. You're observing everything that's going on around you and taking it all in, increasing the amount of data that you're gathering and processing. This all becomes fuel for your intuition.

However, there's more to intuition than just listening to others and watching what they do. Of equal importance in the intuitive process is what you do with your intuition once you have it. If you do nothing, it will quickly evaporate, and you may never see the thought behind it again. Intuition can bring you all sorts of opportunities, but you have to have the courage to trust and act on them, even when the data do not necessarily say that an opportunity is a good one.

The CEO of a major energy corporation explained: "Ignoring them [intuitions] has led to some bad decisions . . . you have to learn to trust your intuition. Otherwise, at the point when you've gathered enough data to be 99.99 percent certain that the decision you're about to make is the correct one, that decision has become obsolete."[4]

As a leader, you should encourage the people in your organization to act on their intuition. You can play a large role in whether your people use their intuition, and then whether they act on it when ideas or opportunities present themselves. You can do this by reinforcing intuition in your company culture and making people feel empowered and safe to use their intuition. And when employees come to you with the ideas and opportunities that their intuition generated, be sure to listen to what they have to say and then adopt as many of these ideas and pursue as many of these opportunities as you reasonably can.

REGULAR PRACTICE WILL STRENGTHEN YOUR INTUITION

Intuition is like any other skill you've got: the more you practice, the better you'll get at it. If you're a baseball player and you don't take time to practice your batting, you're not going to be a good hitter. If you're a golfer and you don't go to the driving range to practice hitting golf balls, you're not going to become the best golfer you can be. Similarly, if you don't practice exercising your intuition, it can get rusty and wither away. Practice will improve your intuitive skills, helping them to become second nature as you regularly exercise them.

We want our associates at Umpqua Bank to be in tune with their customers and to use their intuition and act on it, just like the Ritz-Carlton employee who learned that I would soon be traveling to Morocco and bought and delivered a book about the country. To help encourage our associates to do this, we created a Wow! blog on our company intranet where associates share their stories of wowing our customers with everyone in the company. Stories fall within these seven "superpower" categories:

MegaEar. Listening for and fulfilling even the faintest customer need

Unbeatable Heart. A caring compassion that shines through no matter what

Bankability. Helping customers with banking and protecting them from fraud

Hooray Holler. Loudly and proudly celebrating the great things others do

Presents of Mind. Thinking of a personalized gift that makes someone's day

Helping Hand. Jumping in to assist or rescue someone

Dr. Umpqua. Prescribing the perfect products and services to serve a customer's financial needs

Associates are encouraged to post their stories to share with their fellow associates. Here are a few examples:

"One of our customers locked his keys in his car and was stranded at our bank with no one to come and help him. My manager Zack drove him home to get his keys and brought him back to the bank to finish out the rest of his day!"

"A customer with cerebral palsy who lives on a fixed income was in the store to handle a transaction and mentioned how expensive it was to move. He was sizing down within the same apartment complex, and movers were charging him $500 to move across the street. Store associates stepped in to help, going to the client's apartment to help him pack on a Saturday and then supervising the movers on the following Monday. The store used winnings earned for their team from an internal sales campaign to help pay for the move, even helping to find a handyman to install a safety bar."

"A Commercial Real Estate Team associate visited a customer's office and found an exhausted staff preparing to work all weekend to meet a deadline. Dedicated Umpqua associates purchased a beautiful assortment of snacks (apples, oranges, raspberries, salami, cheese, crackers, candy, water, energy drinks, nut snack packs) to create "baskets," packed them in reusable Umpqua bags, and delivered them to the customer."

"A business customer called to let a store associate know that her husband was diagnosed with a rare form of cancer and that they would be driving some distance for cancer treatments. The associate put together a goodie basket for their trip, purchasing a small cooler and filling it with supplies and water as well as a gas card to help them along their way."

"A customer was completing her transaction at the teller line when she mentioned her birthday was coming up very soon and said nonchalantly that she 'wasn't doing anything too exciting.' Two store associates teamed up to surprise and delight the customer with a balloon, a cake, and a gift card to a local restaurant. The customer was thrilled that her birthday was remembered and shared her cake with the team."

These stories, and many others like them, show that when people are encouraged to be intuitive and then act on their intuition, great things can happen for the organization—and for its people, customers, and communities. It's for this reason that every leader should encourage employees to regularly exercise their intuition.

FOR REFLECTION

- Do you trust your intuition? Do you use your intuition at work? If so, how and when do you use it? If not, what can you do to use it?

- What do you do to exercise your intuition muscles?

- What do you do to encourage your people to use their intuition?

- In what ways do you think your organization might be improved if you encouraged employees to use their intuition?

- In what ways do you use your intuition to identify and act on new opportunities?

Leading Your Organization

Before you are a leader, success is all about growing yourself. When you become a leader, success is all about growing others.
— Jack Welch

Once you learn how to lead yourself, you're ready to lead others. Organizations are complex collections of people, each of whom is following his or her own script and has his or her own dreams, needs, and desires. Your job is to help each of your associates give the very best they have to give and to stay out of their way. Part 2 outlines the essentials of how to execute the basics well, the importance of the value proposition, being available to your people, motivating and inspiring associates, and understanding how to leverage your company's assets.

6

Be Really Good at the Basics

Success is neither magical nor mysterious. Success is the natural consequence of consistently applying the basic fundamentals.
—Jim Rohn

A company is only as good or as strong as the foundation it's built on. In good times, the foundation can act as a catalyst—a stimulant to help move you forward. In difficult times, the foundation becomes a ballast to help keep your organization upright and stable as it faces strong waves of negative change. No matter what business environment you're navigating, you've got to have a strong foundation when it comes to the basics to succeed in the long run. It's no good to try to dazzle customers, current and prospective, with all the amazing new product and service innovations you've got in the pipeline if your people constantly stumble and your systems can't keep up with demand. Before you worry about exceeding your customers' wildest desires, make sure you're fulfilling them first.

If your company is built on stilts, the first minor tremor in business activity could cause it to collapse. So the stronger and the deeper the foundation and the more solidly your organization is cemented to it, the better chance it has to survive even the most difficult times. The strength of this foundation also resonates throughout the organization to your associates, customers, clients, and other stakeholders. And let's face it, a strong foundation doesn't hurt your reputation either.

When you're playing a game of football, if you don't have a front line that can block the opposing players and keep them away from your quarterback, he's going to be ineffective. He won't be able to hand off or pass the ball before he gets clobbered. The members of your company's offensive line have to be able to execute the basics of their job consistently and repeatedly.

For example, if you're a restaurant owner, one of the basics is to pass the government health inspection. Another is that your food has to be pretty good and the interior of your restaurant should be comfortable and draw people to it. Your servers should be friendly, and your customers shouldn't have to wait too long to place their orders and get their food. Those are all basics that people expect to be executed well when they spend their hard-earned money at a restaurant.

If you run a construction company, your customers will expect you to understand how to read blueprints, obtain the permits required to make your construction project legal, and how to hire and manage experienced subcontractors whose work is up to a reasonably high standard. If you can't do these and other construction-related things well, you're not executing the basics.

Every business has a set of basics that it must execute well. Banking is a highly regulated industry, so we have to be very good at all the regulatory requirements that are thrown at us. If we're not, the regulators can stop us from doing business in just the same way that the health department can shut down a restaurant until it complies with the public health laws. This could turn out to be the kiss of death for a restaurant that's already on shaky ground, and many have folded for just this reason. If you're not good at the basics and haven't built a strong, reinforced foundation, you're standing on very shaky ground. One economic downturn or a botched project or two, and your business will quickly be in a fight for its very survival. I can also predict that if you're not good at the basics, you're not going to be any good at the higher-level things that need to be done—those things that will successfully differentiate your company from others like it.

There's one more thing that being good at the basics can do for you: build a reservoir of goodwill and trust with your customers that can carry you through difficult times.

There's a high-end restaurant here in Portland that was named Restaurant of the Year by the *Oregonian* newspaper in 2005. In 2013, it was investigated by Oregon public health officials after more than thirty people who dined at the restaurant over a two-day period developed gastrointestinal symptoms due to an outbreak of a norovirus.[1] Despite the outbreak, which was widely reported in the press, the restaurant bounced back from this potential public relations disaster. Its leadership team acted quickly to address the problem by contacting customers who had dined at the restaurant during the period in question and replacing a refrigerator that wasn't cooling properly. Perhaps even more important, it bounced back because of the reservoir of goodwill that it had banked with its customers and the community over the years.

When asked by local media, the people who had gotten sick said that they weren't worried—that as far as they were concerned, it was still a great restaurant and they were going to go back. If the restaurant hadn't accumulated this goodwill, that would have probably been the end for this particular small business.

So how do you know whether your people are executing the basics well? In my experience, there's only one way to do it: inspecting the work your people are doing on behalf of your business. Because we empower people to do things at Umpqua Bank, there is a very large dose of accountability—and inspection. One of the basics that we absolutely have to execute well is to stay on top of regulatory issues. So I have compliance people, I have regulatory people, I have government affairs people, I have internal audit people, and I have credit review people whose job it is to constantly check to make sure that we're in compliance. In smaller businesses, whoever runs the organization must regularly inspect what's going on. When you delegate responsibility, you have to inspect what your people are doing to make sure that your standards are being lived up to.

COMPANY STANDARDS AND ETHICS

It takes a great deal of self-discipline for leaders to hold the line on their standards and not let them slide. People are coming at you every day to try to tell you why it's okay to look the other way just this once and to let your standards drop below what you consider to be acceptable. If you listen to the constant pounding of that message long enough, you may start to believe it. It takes an incredible amount of self-discipline to say, "No, we're not doing that. We're doing this. This is the way I want it done. I appreciate your input, but we're not going to sacrifice quality and the reputation of our company to get there more quickly."

Years ago I was a guest at the Windsor Court Hotel in New Orleans for a planning session. The hotel is justly famous for its remarkable art collection and its attention to detail. At some point during the proceedings, I was walking down the hallway and went up to one of the hotel's employees to ask directions to the men's room. The employee was at the top of a ladder, dusting the artwork, when I asked him, "Can you tell me where the men's room is?," expecting him to simply point the way. Instead, he said, "Sure," and then he proceeded to climb down from his ladder and personally take me there.

I always wondered why he didn't just stay on that ladder and tell me to go down the hall fifty feet to where the restroom was. I later read in a book that the standards of the Windsor Court Hotel are that employees should never point directions to customers; instead, they are to take customers to their requested destination. That employee could have easily stayed up on his ladder and pointed me to the men's room and I would have been none the wiser. But he took the time and energy to get down off his long ladder and take me there. As a customer of this grand hotel, I was surprised and delighted—it made an impression on me that I still tell people about many years later.

There are all kinds of standards. In our company we have communication standards, professional standards, cultural standards, and more. All of these standards, very important to us, outline to our associates exactly how we expect them to behave and the high level of service we expect them to extend not only to our customers but to one another. I have found that standards need to be in writing; if they aren't, it's too easy to change them on a whim—"I don't like that anymore; I'm going to do it this way." Written standards help people understand what an organization's leadership team wants them to do and how to do it.

But standards are not absolute, and there are times when we want our associates to use their own judgment to decide to do something different. I make a habit of telling people in our company that they're empowered to break the rules if they think it's the right thing to do. But I also let them know that they will be held accountable and that they'll need to be able to explain why they did what they did. Depending on the result, we might say, "Great job, way to go!" or, "That was a good try, but I'd like you to handle it this way next time it comes up." The point is that you must temper your criticism of people for doing what they think is right. You need standards, but you also need your people to use their own discretion when necessary.

Ethics are in essence another kind of standard, albeit a kind that for the most part comes from within an individual rather than being imposed from outside. You want and need to hire ethical people—men and women who know right from wrong, have a strong moral compass, and refuse to break the law. As we saw from the example of Enron, a fundamental failure of ethical behavior and accountability at the top of an organization can put even the most successful company out of business.

An interesting aspect of ethics that's plaguing the largest businesses today is that some of these companies are so large that some people believe they may be too difficult to manage. I don't necessarily believe that, but I do believe an organization can get so big that people are no longer adhering to the standards and ethics that leadership established and believes are being followed. It's difficult to inspect ethical behavior at that size.

Just like a company's culture can be diluted and made weaker the larger it gets, so too can its ethics. Every intangible our company possesses can become diluted for lots of reasons. I think the dilution factor is stronger in larger organizations than in small because there's so much translation going on within the company. The message goes in one end of the organization and may be different by the time it comes out the other side.

The leader has to be the person in the organization who looks most critically at it—that's part of the job. How else can you get better if your leader doesn't think you can get better? When it comes to ethics and the standards you have to be able to inspect, you must be able to hold people accountable; you always must be trying to improve and make them stronger and to develop methods, systems, and processes that enable you to track these behaviors. And this is just as important in small companies as it is in big ones.

CORE VALUES OF THE LEADERSHIP TEAM

When we talk about the core values and the leadership team, there's one that is absolutely fundamental: you must walk the walk and talk the talk. We have two sets of eyes watching us—those we work for and those who work for us. And the people who work for us are the most important set of eyes because if we're not providing resources for them and living up to the standards and the ethics and the cultural foundation that the company was founded on, if we're shrugging off things that we feel are important, if we're rolling our eyes on important things in front of people, we're sending a loud and clear message that these things aren't important. So if you as a leader don't consider ethical behavior or your company's culture or core values to be important, then your people probably won't either.

I'm personally much more patient with people in the field screwing something up than I am with an executive back at the home office. We pay our executives well, so it's fair to expect them to be really good at what they do. They know what the rules are. They know our standards and the ethics, and I expect them to live up to them. But sometimes they don't, and when our fellow associates observe this behavior, it reflects badly on all of us. We have to set the example, since there could be hundreds of associates who will think that if our standards aren't important to them, then they aren't important to the rest of us. Whether it's intentional or not, I'll call them on the carpet if they're doing anything that might weaken the cultural standards of our company. I won't tolerate that. It's a zero-tolerance situation—there's just no room for messing around with our company's culture and our high standards.

BELIEVE IN YOURSELF

There are two aspects to believing in yourself. The first is that you have to have confidence in your ability to accomplish your goals. That's contagious. Remember: people are watching. The other is that you as a leader need to buy into whatever it is that your company represents. You also need complete buy-in from your leadership team. They have to believe in it. They've got to walk the walk, talk the talk, look the look, dress the dress, and fully support your company's culture, standards, and values. If they don't, you have the wrong leaders on your team.

This buy-in goes hand in hand with believing in yourself, and it's just as important. If you say, "I believe I'm really good at my job, but I think what's going on here at the company stinks," then you're going to fail. And if you say, "I really like what's going on at the company, but I stink at doing my job," you're also going to fail. But if you're in the enviable position of being able to say, "I believe strongly in what's going on in the company *and* I know I can do my job well," your chances of success are significantly improved. It's not enough to just believe in yourself. You also need to believe in your organization and what it stands for and represents.

And as a leader, not only do you need to believe in the importance of executing the basics well; you have to believe that you can support and hold your people accountable for executing them. One way to look at executing the basics well is that you're helping to build a solid brick foundation that will last for decades or maybe even centuries into the future. For a company to thrive that long, you've got to build that foundation well, with bricks fired from the company's core values and in the execution of the basics. If you're not going to live up to your company's culture, standards, and values, the bricks in your foundation will start to crumble, and your company, which was built to last, will eventually collapse from within.

When the recession hit the banking industry in 2008, the management team at Umpqua decided that we wanted to come out of the recession with a stronger balance sheet than when we entered it. To some observers at the time, this was unbelievable. Many people were saying, "Let's just hunker down and *survive*." But my reply was, "No, I don't want Umpqua to just survive. I want our company to thrive. I know we're going to take some lumps along the way and that's the way it goes, but

I want us to come out of this with a stronger balance sheet." And in fact, as of this writing, our balance sheet is indeed stronger than it was in 2007 and 2008. It's so strong that I often tell our people that should another financial disaster hit the United States where banks are in big trouble again, sure, we'll probably lose a few bricks in the foundation we've worked so hard to build and strengthen, but the walls will stand and we'll weather the storm, no matter how severe it may turn out to be.

It's a good feeling to be able to tell your people this, and it goes a long way to build both the comfort they currently feel in their jobs and the confidence they feel for the future of the bank—and themselves.

FOR REFLECTION

- What are the basics of your business? What are the fundamental things you need to get done?

- Does your business execute the basics well? Why or why not?

- What are the standards in your company that you are willing to relax? Why? Which standards do you refuse to let slide? Why?

- What are the core values of your leadership team, and are they consistent with your company's culture and values?

7

The Value of a Value Proposition

I have always believed, and I still believe, that whatever good or bad fortune may come our way we can always give it meaning and transform it into something of value.
—Hermann Hesse

The term *value proposition* is thrown around a lot in business today. Almost every company claims to have one, but few people who run or work within them actually know what it is; in fact, they don't have a clue. In my mind, if a company's people don't know what its value proposition is, then it doesn't have one. To me, a value proposition is the sum total of the various ways that you differentiate your company and your products and services so people want to do business with you. I don't care if you sell Levi's jeans, table tennis balls, or Christmas trees—it doesn't make any difference. People need a good reason to do business with you.

If the products and services you offer aren't yet commodities, there's a danger that people that may see them as such. And when that happens, they make their buying decisions primarily or solely on price, not on the other things you offer. The way to prevent this from happening is to create a value proposition that demonstrates clearly to customers the extra value that your products and services provide that none of your competitors offer.

This is especially true in the financial industry. Unfortunately, it's the rare bank that has spent the energy, time, and focus required to create a meaningful value proposition. The only thing these businesses can rely on is price, and in my experience, that's a losing game. Most of these companies don't know it, but at some point they will hit a brick wall, and that will be the end of the road for them. There are definitely exceptions to this, particularly in the case of companies that have a huge scale. But relatively few companies have that level of scale.

PRICE IS A DEATH SPIRAL

Companies that compete primarily on price are in great danger of stepping into the quicksand of a death spiral where consumers are always shopping for the best deal, and the relationship they can build with a business doesn't matter much to them. I think about a company like Hewlett-Packard that tried to get into the personal computer business in a big way by acquiring Compaq. Unfortunately, it ended up getting stuck in a near-death spiral as it was forced to drop prices and got caught in a race to the bottom. HP still sells personal computers, but its leaders know that there isn't much of a future in it. The future, its leaders have decided, is in enterprise software, where the products are not caught in the commodity trap and the margins are much more favorable to the company's bottom line.

The simple fact for smaller companies is that whatever you're selling, the big guys can outprice you anytime they feel like it. The same thing is true with banks. To thrive—and to survive—you've got to have a better value proposition than the big guys.

LIVING YOUR VALUE PROPOSITION

When it comes to a value proposition, a lot of companies make a big deal about having one, but they don't bother to live it. It's the same thing that often happens with companies and their mission statements. Someone in the company takes the time to write it, and then the company frames it and puts it on the wall. But as soon as it goes on the wall, it's forgotten. A lot of people do the same thing with their value proposition.

A value proposition is good only if people understand it, practice it, are held accountable to it, develop a passion for it, and can tangibly and actively see how it works and makes a difference in their business. When this happens, it creates the wind that drives everyone forward and can be measured. A value proposition is something that you use every day to differentiate your company from the competition.

When people go to Walmart, they know why they're going to do business there: the low prices on the things that they regularly buy. On the opposite end of the scale, people know why they want to do business with the Ritz-Carlton: they're going to be treated increasingly well and they're willing to pay for that. I believe that everyone will pay for quality up to a point. While I might pay five dollars for a quality loaf of bread, I'm not going to spend fifty dollars for the same loaf. Similarly, people are willing to pay a dollar or two to buy a cold soda or water from a beverage machine, but they won't pay ten dollars for it. People will pay for quality and service, but you better deliver. If they ever feel they're not getting the value they expected, it could be the last time they buy from you.

The value proposition sets you apart from the rest of the pack. In a tough economy like the one we've been going through and that this book is focused on, the question is this: How do you get through the difficult and uncertain times and get on with life? A meaningful value proposition is probably the most important thing you have in your arsenal to motivate and stimulate your company to get through challenging times.

CREATING YOUR VALUE PROPOSITION

Umpqua's value proposition was created out of our culture, and over time it became part of who we are. But our value proposition didn't just appear out of nowhere: we had to create it.

I'm a bit of a contrarian when it comes to some of the standard management rules that are taught in business school. I believe, for example, that if your value proposition is a good one from the start, then you should be able to ride it through good weather and bad. That doesn't mean you don't tweak it from time to time to optimize it for the market conditions in which you find yourself. But you can't be a fair-weather supporter of the value proposition. You can't and you shouldn't change it every time the business environment changes. Your value proposition is something you should stand up for come hell or high water.

Not long ago, I was invited to go on a sales call with one of our loan officers. Before we arrived at the place of business, my guys were peppering me with the deal terms of the loan and what our competitor, a large bank, was offering. They told me that we were going to have to tighten up our deal to meet the pricing that the other institution had presented. During the conversation, I finally said, "Stop, stop. You guys should know that I am not going to talk price with this prospect. I don't need to understand the loan terms. I know you do, and you should be able to work out the details." They looked at me with a concerned look on their faces, and I'm sure they thought to themselves, *Oh, no, this guy's going to lose this deal for us!*

When the meeting started and after we made introductions all around, I asked the company executives a simple question. Keep in mind that this was all taking place in the middle of the recession with the housing market crashing all around us and that our prospective customer manufactured a product specific to that industry. Despite the downturn, the company was continuing to do well. So I asked, "It's great to see how well your company is doing considering the economic situation we all find ourselves in, and I'm curious what you attribute your success to. Is it because your product is inexpensive and it's easy to swap out when it wears out, producing multiple sales? Or is it because it's a top-of-the-line product to start with, and the product and service reputation you've built over the years is so good"?

In reality, I was asking them, "What's your value proposition?"

One of their executives was quick to answer. He said, "No, Ray, we're not the least expensive. We don't believe in that strategy. What has sustained us during good and bad times is the simple fact that we produce a very high-end product that our customers trust is reliable. We couple that with a level of installation support and after-sales customer experience that we believe our competitors will not and cannot equal. We don't believe in being cheap. We do believe in quality and producing a product we are proud of."

When he finished, I looked at him and said, "Welcome to Umpqua Bank."

"What do you mean?" he asked.

"You just described our company," I replied. "Like your company, we're not the K-Mart of banks either. Like you, we believe in quality. Like you, we understand that we have to be price competitive, but our service levels, commitment to our communities, and unique delivery system provide great value that should never be discounted. We agree that your value proposition of building a quality product that you're proud of and standing behind makes an incredible difference. You know it's worth the extra money that your clients are paying."

"You're absolutely correct," said the executive.

"That's where we stand," I explained. "And we look forward to welcoming you to the world's greatest bank, Umpqua Bank."

I walked out of the room with my loan officer close behind me. He appreciated my attendance, and we felt confident about earning the company's business. As we got back into the car, I told him, "There's a lesson to be learned here. A quality company with quality people and products doesn't have to be the least expensive to obtain new business. During sales calls, you should always lead with what our value proposition and company culture mean to our clients. Leading with price cheapens our company and places you in a position where the only topic you will be able to discuss is price and terms. The larger banks can always outprice us if they choose. What they can't do is outdeliver us. Focus on that, and I guarantee you'll increase your loan portfolio fast."

I'm constantly reinforcing this message with our loan people: when you go talk with people about our products or services, the first thing you should be talking about is not price. You should be talking about the quality of our company and our products and the strength that stands behind them. When you do that, you're telling people what type of company we are. And if they recognize and can appreciate the value that you provide, they're likely to pay for it.

This is what separates you from everybody else who's walking in there saying, "Well, if Umpqua Bank is at 5 percent, then we'll do 4.5." What kind of business is that? Not one that I want to be in.

A lot of research is done each year on value propositions. And when the consultants come in, they say that before you create a value proposition, you need to make sure you know and understand your customers and your competition. I'm sure there's value in getting all that information, but as many times as they do that—and we've done that at Umpqua Bank—I believe that those things don't drive the value proposition. For me, it's more about what I want to accomplish with my company. How do I want to do business, and what do I stand for?

If you go out and ask your customers what they would like your products to be or to do, they often don't know. They do know they want you to remain competitive and continue to provide them with the products and support they need. They want you to continue to provide more of the same. So it's less about what the *competition* is doing and it's more about what *you* want to do. What can you do to continue to execute the basics well and deliver on your value proposition? And as you're delivering on these promises to your customers, what can you do to occasionally surprise and delight them—to continue to move your organization and its products and services and the way you deliver them forward?

That said, there is a right way and a wrong way to build a value proposition. Summarizing the work of marketing and sales optimizers MarketingExperiments Lab, Peep Laja offers the following list of characteristics that make a good value proposition:

- Clarity! It's easy to understand.

- It communicates the concrete results a customer will get from purchasing and/or using your products and services.

- It says how it's different or better than the competitor's offer.

- It avoids hype (like "never seen before amazing miracle product"), superlatives ("best"), and business jargon ("value-added interactions").

- It can be read and understood in about five seconds.

- Also, in most cases, there is a difference between the value proposition for your company and your product. You must address both.[1]

Living your value proposition requires that your people buy into it. And to get your people to buy into it, you've got to communicate it and hold them accountable to reinforce it. It may require tough love over a sustained period of time to create a value proposition that you want to make happen, but the results will be worth it.

Everybody hates regrettable turnover or when good people leave the company for whatever reason. Good people are the core of your company, and you shouldn't let them get away easily. If an associate has an opportunity to leave but is fully engaged in her work, then you should fight hard to retain her. On the flip side of the coin, if you have someone who isn't a believer in what you're doing, he or she needs to get out of the way. People who don't buy into your approach of doing business become contagious and can carry a virus that will quickly spread throughout your company and kill everything you're trying to do. And even with good people, every now and then you've got to go back and make sure that they're still plugged in.

COMMUNICATING YOUR VALUE PROPOSITION

In challenging times, the value proposition keeps muscle on the bone—something people can have faith in that will get them through the difficulties. If the value proposition is a meaningful one, you can create a lot of loyalty and momentum with it.

So how do you best communicate that to your clients, your customers? You have to tell your customers—and your community and other stakeholders—what you stand for. I find it interesting that salespeople expect you to want to talk about the pricing and the discount and the FOB point when what most people should be talking about instead is the quality of their organization. If you're doing a presentation, you would say something like this, "Here's why you need to buy from us." This often answers the question they're thinking about anyway, which is, "Why should I buy from these guys?"

Two common pitfalls of value propositions are not having one at all and having a value proposition but not knowing what it is. For example, if I were to walk into ten bank presidents' offices and ask them to tell me what their value proposition is, I'll bet you that the majority of them would say something along the lines of, "We're locally owned and operated," and, "We provide great service." But that's what everybody else says as well, so it's not a differentiator with customers. In fact, comments like that have lost their meaning and importance to customers. What's worse, the bank president says the bank provides good service, and when you ask him or her to provide you with some quantitative measure of that good service, that same presidents will look at you like you're nuts.

You need something that makes your company stand out, and it must be meaningful for it to register with your customers and your potential customer.

The culture of Umpqua is built around empowering people to do incredible things—anything they want to do to enhance our customer's experience with us. Our culture has been built around the empowerment we've given our associates. It also includes a healthy dose of accountability. Our value proposition was born out of a culture we've created over the past eighteen years. It's proven to be an incredible asset for us and one that allows us to compete on more than price. A meaningful value proposition creates just that: value not only to the company but to the companies that you're speaking with. A good value proposition takes a company's culture and puts it into action. It's what makes a company's culture come to life: people can see it, touch it, and appreciate it.

If you're in the business of selling a commodity like groceries or computers, the value proposition becomes even more important because you're selling the same thing all your competitors are. And if you have a small- or medium-sized business and you think you can stand out using price, you're dreaming. In Umpqua's case, our value proposition was built on empowerment and accountability, but it came out of a process. I like to think of it in the same terms as a murder mystery. When the police are trying to narrow down suspects, they do so through a process of elimination. The question is not who did it. The question is who *didn't* do it. The last guy standing is usually the bad guy.

When I came to Umpqua, the question was, How do I differentiate the bank from my competition? I can't outprice the big guys, I can't out-resource them, and I can't out-computer them. But what I could do through this last-guy-standing process was out-deliver them because I'm more agile, I'm smaller, I can move more quickly, and I can do things that would be impossible for them to do. And that, combined with empowerment and accountability, became the value proposition of our company.

NURTURING YOUR VALUE PROPOSITION

If you grow only for the sake of growth and don't continue to nurture your culture and your value proposition, they will most certainly erode. As your company gets bigger, bureaucracy has the tendency to raise its ugly head and take over. Before you know what hit you, you're just like all the other larger nondescript companies where process rules. In Umpqua's case, it's taken a lot of work to grow our company so rapidly. What's more important is that at the same time, we were strengthening our culture and value proposition to make us what we are today. To ignore these areas would have been devastating for Umpqua. It would have been admitting defeat and failure since we would have sacrificed all that hard work and lost what has differentiated us from our competition.

We have an expression here at Umpqua; it's called "big bank creep," which is the process where a nimble small bank that cares about its customers becomes rigid and bureaucratic and succumbs to processes. We fight like hell to prevent it from creeping in unnoticed when we're not paying attention. It comes at us all the time and from every direction, and inspires us to be diligent in protecting our culture. We have something on our intranet called UmpquaSmart, which enables associates to let us know when they encounter a policy or process that's killing the pulse of the company. It's preventive medicine that unfortunately insurance companies don't pay for.

FOR REFLECTION

- Does your company have a value proposition? If so, what is it? If not, why not?

- Do you live your value proposition, or is it filed away and forgotten? What is the impact on your organization and your customers?

- Does your value proposition have all the characteristics that make a value proposition great?

- How do you communicate your value proposition to your customers, your people, and your other stakeholders? How can this communication be improved?

8

Be Available

The Lord doesn't ask about your ability, only your availability; and, if you prove your dependability, the Lord will increase your capability.
—Unknown

As a leader, you should always be available to your people, your customers, and your community. This is even more important when times are tough. When you disappear from view, people begin to worry, and when they begin to worry, they become distracted from the work at hand. Your organization will perform better when you're visible and available and exude confidence.

There are two ways to look at being available. One is that it means you're accessible, that both your associates and the public are able to contact you directly. The other is that it means not hiding from your constituents when times get tough. In fact, I believe that when the economy is bad and your business environment is getting more and more uncertain, this is the time when you as a leader need to be even more available and visible than you have been—and not just to your employees, but to your suppliers, public, media, bankers, associates, and customers.

When the business environment is uncertain, your people, your customers, your partners and your other stakeholders want to be reassured that you're on top of things and that everything is going to be all right. But if you're hard to contact or reach, people tend to worry about what could possibly be going on. If they can't get an explanation or reassurance from a company's leadership team about what's happening, fear sets in. This type of fear—the fear of the unknown—is unproductive and often creates negative rumors as people make up their own reasons to explain issues.

If I'm a customer and can't get in touch with the company that I buy something from—no one will answer the phone or return my calls or respond to my e-mails—that company is sending a powerful signal that communicates something negative to customers. They begin to fill in the blanks, imagining that your company is in trouble or you don't feel your customers are important. If you respond, at minimum they'll understand what's going on; it could have been as simple as your phone systems being down. By not being available, you're allowing them to answer for you, and their answers can often be quite imaginative, inaccurate, and not in the best interests of your company. Whatever the issue is, you owe them an explanation, and it's in your best interest to give it.

It's easier to be available when times are good. Everybody wants to tell the world how great they're doing, but when things aren't so hot, people too often have the tendency to disappear or hide. You may unintentionally be sending out a message that will eventually come back to haunt you.

KEEP YOUR ORGANIZATION FLAT

At Umpqua, our organization is as flat as we can make it. This is because I believe that the fewer levels of management you have, the better you are. We don't need to create obstacles for our people to jump over in order to get to decision makers. Too many companies have so many layers of management that their organization chart looks like a pyramid, where only those with incredible tenacity can communicate with the top. When you have a flat organization, it's usually much easier for others to get answers to questions and resolve problems, and allows management to take advantage of opportunities that the company can benefit from. It also keeps management connected to your customers, an essential part of delivering extraordinary service.

When asked by a reporter some years ago who he thought was the greatest leader in the United States, management guru Peter Drucker didn't hesitate. Frances Hesselbein, he replied, at the time CEO of the Girl Scouts of the USA. When the reporter balked at Drucker's answer, insisting that surely he meant the best nonprofit leader in the United States, Drucker wasn't dissuaded from his assessment. He retorted, "Frances Hesselbein could manage any company in America."

In his Foreword to *Hesselbein on Leadership*, Jim Collins explained how Frances described the flat organization that she devised for the Girl Scouts. According to Collins,

> In 1976, Hesselbein found herself at the center of an organization cascading into irrelevance. I'm careful here not to say, "atop" the organization, as Frances would never think of her role that way. When describing her organization structure to a *New York Times* reporter, she put a glass at the center of a lunch table and created a set of concentric

circles radiating outward—plates, cups, saucers—
connected by knives, forks, and spoons. "I'm here," she
said, pointing to the glass in the middle. "I'm not on top
of anything."[1]

Using this unique flat organization approach to management,
Hesselbein rebuilt the Girl Scouts organization, increasing
its membership to 2.25 million girls and a mostly volunteer
workforce of 780,000 people.[2]

Too many layers of management serve as unnecessary translators, and messages too often get changed or lost altogether
by the time they make their way through the organization.
Umpqua is purposely designed to be flat because I want people
to get answers quickly, and I don't want or need translators. I
want people to have confidence that management is available to
them and that we want and value what they have to say on company issues and opportunities. This has an incredibly positive
impact on our associates' morale, their confidence, the level
of service they provide, and the way they communicate to our
customers and other stakeholders. I understand that at times, a
flat leadership structure might not be the most efficient way of
managing an organization, but my intuition tells me that this
is the best way.

When I talk about being available, that doesn't necessarily mean waiting for the phone to ring or for an e-mail
to come in. It's being proactive about being available that
counts. I received a letter from one of our associates in the
Puget Sound area. The letter wasn't actually addressed to me,
but someone thought I might get a kick out of reading it and
forwarded it to me. In her letter, the associate wrote about
how much she loves working for Umpqua Bank. As soon as

I finished reading it, I picked up the phone and called her. I said, "I hope you don't mind that I saw your letter, but after reading it, I just wanted to call to tell you that your comments were terrific and let you know how much I appreciate your passion for Umpqua." She was happy I read her letter and surprised that I called to tell her what her thoughts meant to me. As you can imagine, that simple act of being available to my associates went a long way with her.

On the first of every month, I sign about 250 cards for associates who are celebrating their annual anniversary with the organization during that month. Every year everyone gets a card from me that tells them how much I appreciate them, their commitment to the company, and our standards for delivering customer service. And I sincerely do. I also make a point of getting out and visiting our stores and departments often so our associates can see the whites of my eyes. They need to have the opportunity to visit with and talk to me. I need to be available.

BE AVAILABLE TO EVERYONE: ASSOCIATES, CUSTOMERS, SUPPLIERS, AND THE PUBLIC

Being available can be easy to do. One way I make myself available to our associates and customers is through what we call the "Ray Phone." Each of our bank stores has a special phone. When people select the number 8 on the keypad, their calls are connected directly to me here in Portland. When I'm at my desk, I answer these calls myself. If I'm not at my desk and a caller leaves a message, I make a point of returning the call on the same day. When we put those phones into place back when we had only six bank stores, I had no idea the impact it was going to have. It wasn't a big deal at the time—I was just letting people in the small town of Roseburg, Oregon, know that I was around and looked forward to talking with them.

Today I average one or two calls a week. It used to be only two or three a month, but our customers seem to like the fact that they can talk with the CEO of their bank. For the most part, they call just to let me know how much they enjoy the uniqueness of our stores and how much they appreciate our staff. They're also impressed that if they choose to, they can talk to the CEO of the company. Many of the calls I get are people, who after I say, "Hello," just say something like, "Never mind. I just wanted to see if you would really answer the phone," and then they hang up. Or sometimes they'll ask me, "Is this really Ray Davis?" Our customers rarely use the phones to call me with problems, but when they do, I make sure we get them fixed right away. I'm available.

And it makes a difference. For example, a customer called me from one of the phones; we had a nice conversation and he was complimentary about the people he was dealing with at his local store. I thanked him for his comments and shortly after the call sent a note to the store staff thanking them for their good work. About three weeks later, I got another call from the same guy. He said, "Ray, I don't mean to bother you, but I just had to call you to tell you this story."

I said, "Sure, what's up?"

He said, "Well, you know how two or three weeks ago, I gave you a call, and you answered the phone and we had a great chat. I just want you to know it really meant a lot to me."

"I was happy to talk with you," I replied. "I'm glad you called."

He then continued his story. "I was so impressed that I decided to test this on another bank. Since I also had a checking account with one of the large national banks in town, I decided to see if I could get their CEO on the phone as well. I wanted to find out if I could get through to him the same way I got through to you."

"How'd it go?" I asked, although I suspected that I already knew the answer.

"Not good," the caller replied. "It took me about a week and a half just to get through to the floor in the building where the CEO works. And when I finally got one of his two or three assistants on the phone and said, 'I'd like to speak to the CEO,' the answer I got from the assistant was, 'Mr. Smith [not his real name] does not take calls from the public. Have a good day.' And then she hung up on me."

You won't be surprised that we picked up the rest of this caller's business. I'm always happy to talk with him or anyone else who takes the time to pick up the phone in one of our stores to give me a call.

I know that all CEOs are very busy people. I'm busy too. But I always have a minute or two in my workday to pick up the phone and say hello to one of my customers. I think it's a mistake for people in my position not to make themselves available to their customers, their people, and the community at large.

HOW ELSE CAN YOU LEAD IN DIFFICULT TIMES?

If a business is going through a tough period, and associates are wondering, "How are we going to get through this?" not having access to the decision makers—whoever they may be—creates a large amount of uncertainty and fear. My guess is that there's a high likelihood that many of those associates, when given the opportunity to land somewhere else, are going to be gone. As important as it is for leaders to be available in good times, this is especially important when times are tough.

It's a natural reaction for a leader to hunker down when things are looking bad and circle the wagons: constantly meet with the top leadership team, while unintentionally neglecting the company's other associates. Not only do associates feel left out of the loop as a result, but their leaders aren't hearing from them on important matters. These people may have great ideas about things the company could do to get through its difficulties, but these great ideas go unheard and are not acted on when the decision makers are hunkered down in a bunker and out of sight.

Why not have your associates be part of the solution? They'll feel more worthwhile and more valuable to the company, more engaged, and they'll understand that you respect them and their opinions. What's wrong with that? Most businesses have a lot of very smart people working for them, many of whom have great ideas. When I look for new ideas that could differentiate our company from our competitors I often get important and timely input from our associates. In some cases, we're able to implement the ideas as our associates suggest them; in others, we implement them after we modify them to the specifics of our business. To me, being available to our people is more than just answering the phone when someone calls; it's about engaging with our people in good times and bad.

Engaging your people is important for any leader to do. The Gallup Organization keeps close tabs on the engagement of millions of American workers in their jobs—that is, how connected they feel to their workplaces. In its most recent survey of American businesses, Gallup found that only 30 percent of American workers—less than one-third—are engaged in their jobs, working with passion, and feeling a profound connection to their company. And if that's not bad enough, Gallup also found that 52 percent of American workers are not engaged in their jobs. They're "checked out" and just going through the motions at work. But here's the really bad news: The remaining 18 percent of employees—about one in every five—are actively disengaged from their jobs. Not only are they not happy at work, they are actively working against the goals of their employers, undermining the good work that their engaged coworkers accomplish.[3]

BE CONFIDENT; BE REAL

If you're available to your people but not motivating or helping them get through the problem at hand, what makes you think you're going to get through it? Being available is one thing, but if you're in a position of leadership, people expect you to lead, expect you to have ideas, expect you to be confident, and expect you to take action.

It's okay to let your people know that you don't have all the answers. But they need to feel confident that you are willing to listen to them and then act to get through the rough patch your company may be experiencing. This confidence becomes contagious, which is clearly positive. You have to demonstrate confidence and at the same time be truthful and transparent about the issues at hand while you make yourself available.

I often remind my executives that we sometimes take for granted the impact we have on the people who work for us, both positive and negative. A phone call, a personal office visit, a sincere thank-you in the hallway: each of these interactions and more can significantly change the course of an associate's day. When I personally called the young woman who wrote the letter expressing how good she felt working for Umpqua Bank, it cost me nothing and yet she was pleasantly surprised. I'm sure she told others about the call, and I hope it was a positive experience for her and for her fellow associates. The opportunity to have such a lasting impact on people makes a big difference in their work lives and can make a difference in the lives of the executives who take the time to reach out.

FOR REFLECTION

- Are you available to your people, your customers, and your community and other stakeholders? In what ways, and how often?

- What can you do to improve your availability?

- Would flattening your organization improve communication and decision making? How, and in what ways?

- What are you doing to engage your people in their jobs?

9

Motivate and Inspire

Of course motivation is not permanent. But then, neither is
bathing; but it is something you should do on a regular basis.
—Zig Ziglar

I tell people at Umpqua that if you're a leader, then your job
description is really the same as mine. I don't care if you
lead one person or one thousand, your job description has just
two simple words: *motivate* and *inspire*. If you can't motivate
and inspire people, you can't lead. It's as simple as that. If you
can't motivate and inspire others, then you need to get out
of the way and make room for someone who can. Doing this
requires building trust and unlocking the energy and passion
inside every one of us. And it means making a conscious effort
every day to recognize and reward the kinds of behaviors you
want from your people.

Before I got into banking, I was an officer in the military.
If I was going to get my platoon motivated to do something
challenging, I knew the approach I shouldn't take:

Okay guys, we've got to take this hill. Now, the enemy isn't going to make it easy for us. In fact, he's going to make it very difficult. It's going to be bloody; it's going to be hell. Not only that, but half of us probably won't come back—maybe less. I don't know why we've got to take this particular hill, but the general gave me orders to do it, so let's just do our jobs and hope for the best.

I can guarantee that no one would get fired up for that weak attempt at motivating my platoon. Would you?

But if I had put things in perspective and painted a vision of what we were going to do, exactly why we were going to do it, and why it was important to my fellow soldiers, our families, and our nation as a whole that we accomplish our goal—no matter how difficult it might be—then that would be a very different situation. My troops would be motivated, perhaps even fired up, to storm that hill and push out the enemy occupying it.

SINCERITY, TRUST, AND PASSION

In my experience, one of the most important traits of successful leaders is sincerity. If you're going to motivate and inspire your people, you have to build trust and you have to be sincere. If you were to get a bunch of leaders in the room and ask them, "What is it that you were you trying to do today?" I think that most of them would probably agree that what they've been trying to do is persuade people to do something. But persuasion is just one part of the equation. Leaders who are able to motivate and inspire their associates to do the things they need them to do are going to be successful—they're going to move their organizations in the right direction.

If you're a leader and you can't motivate and inspire your associates, then you're dead in the water. Unfortunately the majority of employees in American businesses today don't feel that they're being recognized for their efforts, and as a result, they're not as motivated and inspired as they could be. Research conducted by employee motivation and incentives company Maritz reveals that 34 percent of employees disagree or disagree strongly that they're recognized in ways that are meaningful to them. Surprisingly, just 12 percent of employees strongly agree that they're consistently recognized in ways they value.[1]

According to employee recognition expert Bob Nelson, "One of the strongest tools in a business's arsenal for increasing motivation is recognition."[2] Nelson defines *recognition* as "a positive consequence provided to a person for a desired behavior or result." He goes on to describe what recognition looks like:

> Recognition can take the form of acknowledgment, approval, or the expression of gratitude. It means appreciating someone for something he or she has done for you, your group, or your organization. It can also come in the form of asking someone's opinion, involving them in a decision, or encouraging them in their career. Recognition can be given while an employee is striving to achieve a certain goal or behavior, or once he or she has completed it.[3]

Additional research that Maritz conducted shows that employees who receive recognition where they work are:

- Five times more likely to feel valued
- Seven times more likely to stay with the company

- Six times more likely to invest in the company

- Eleven times more likely to feel completely committed to the company[4]

As a leader, I can't make you get behind me; I can't make you follow me. I've got to get you to *want* to get behind me. There's a huge difference between ordering someone to get in line versus explaining the positive benefits to the associate and the organization and its customers by doing so.

One more thing: when you're motivating and inspiring others as a leader, you have to be contagious. If you have the passion, the enthusiasm, and the ability to motivate and inspire people and if all these things become contagious, then you'll have an organization that's on fire. I haven't met a person yet who doesn't have passion about something. It might be helping customers, or reading mystery novels, or fishing, or spending time with loved ones. Great leaders tap into the passion people already have within themselves. Everyone wants to do a good job and please others. Effective leaders recognize this fact, and they find ways to motivate and inspire associates to unleash this desire to perform well.

And it's a two-way street. Just as leaders can motivate and inspire their associates, so too can an organization's associates motivate and inspire its leaders. You see this when leaders get standing ovations from their workers. The message, "We're in it. We get it. We're with you," is remarkably motivating and inspiring to leaders. It communicates loud and clear that the leader is trusted, and his or her people think he or she can do it. If I'm successful in motivating and inspiring my people, then they should also be successful in motivating and inspiring me. And when it comes back at you like that, it's a big deal. It's *huge*.

THE VALUE OF PEOPLE IN UNCERTAIN TIMES

In uncertain moments or times, people look for support, encouragement, and help. This includes leaders, who want their advisors around them. It's a natural human trait that we reach out to others, and it's a good thing we do. I'm sure there are people who feel, "No, this is my problem. I'm going to deal with it." This attitude, however, can be counterproductive and even dangerous to their health. People need to remember that the moment you put your problem on the table, it's easier to put it in perspective and the healing or resolution process can begin. If you're keeping it inside yourself and worry about what to do, it could burn a hole in your stomach! This attitude won't be conducive to making progress and at best is not productive. And that's not healthy for a company or a person.

People have the opportunity to be resource catalysts for helping leaders, managers, and family members work through issues. I'm not an island. I'm not in this thing all by myself.

When I think about Umpqua Bank, I often say the most valuable asset we possess is our culture, because our culture has been created by our people. In 2008–2009, when the recession was creating havoc for our industry, including our bank, I continued to reach out. I needed good people by my side.

There's another element of this too: these people—especially those who feel supported by family or friends or their company—are the people with the freedom to give advice. Providing more empowerment to them and then giving them the ability to provide constructive criticism is motivating and keeps them involved in the process.

An important way to keep our people involved and motivated to advance our company is our focus group meetings where I get ten to twelve of my fellow associates—no one from management—to sit down with me for an hour and just talk about how the company could be better. In these meetings, I'm actively looking for constructive criticism. The only rule I have in these meetings is we're not going to talk about people problems. We're focused on talking about how we make this company better from our associates' point of view. The input I get from these meetings is incredible, and I act on the good ideas I get from them immediately. Of course, not all the ideas are good ones. That's okay, and it's a natural part of the focus group process. If that's the case, then I tell them that's probably something we won't be looking into, but I'm truthful with them and don't get their hopes up when an idea isn't going to be implemented.

How else can a company get better if it's not willing to listen to constructive criticism, if it's not willing to listen to what it's not doing as well as it could? If you're not willing to listen, you're not going to improve and you're not going to grow. That's not a recipe for success for any leader.

THE VALUE OF TEAM PLAYERS

The value of an organization's team is incalculable, and it's limited only by the amount of energy, focus, and passion it can unleash. When I took on my job at the helm of Umpqua Bank, I quickly realized that I couldn't change the organization by myself. I couldn't possibly be everywhere all the time, especially if the company was growing. So in the early 1990s we created the President's Club, whose members are cultural ambassadors for Umpqua Bank. These are team players; people for whom confidence, motivation, and the unique Umpqua culture are contagious.

At the same time, the members of the President's Club aren't afraid to provide constructive criticism when we're less than the best we can be, to make sure that we continue to get better. Today the President's Club has about 125 members scattered throughout the organization. They are my eyes and ears, and I meet with them every quarter.

Within the President's Club, we have a chairman's committee made up of a small group of President's Club members, with one person designated the chairperson. This group meets on a fairly regular basis to talk about where we're going from here, what we need to do, and what we need to get better at as a company. This team is a tremendous asset for us. I'd like to think that I have the ability to motivate and inspire the people I come in contact with, but I can't come in contact with everybody every day. The members of the President's Club are my ambassadors, and the group has proven to be invaluable to me.

The President's Club promotes the Umpqua culture, and has a variety of ways to recognize teams that are doing a great job. For example, they give out the Team Award. (The members of the President Club do this independently, by themselves; I have nothing to do with it.) They select the team that they believe is living up to the standards of our company in the most professional way. It could be a team in one of our bank stores, it could be a department, it could be a division of a department, or any other organizational element. Winning the Team

Award is important to our associates, and the President's Club is empowered to award it any way that they want to.

Any associate is eligible for membership in the President's Club, and anyone in the company can nominate anyone else to be in the club. The nominations go to a selection committee of club members. They take the nominations and reduce them to six people in each of two different regions: one includes Oregon and Washington, and the other includes California and Nevada. The President's Club in each of these regions votes for their top three candidates, and those who are on 75 percent of the ballots are inducted.

That all makes it sound like it's easy to get into the President's Club, but it's not. In fact, in 2013 we inducted a young man who had been with the company for ten years and on the ballot for probably five or six of those ten years. The members of the club enjoy a lot of prestige along with their memberships. They're granted some company stock, special name tags, and other perks. The club is very important to our associates and to me.

Associates serve on the President's Club for ten years. When that term is up, they are moved to the President's Club Advisory Council; in other words, they become President's Club emeriti. This allows us to constantly bring new blood and new people into the President's Club.

What we're trying to do with things like the President's Club is ensure that no matter what size we become as an organization, our culture grows faster. As long as our culture remains strong—what we consider to be the most valuable asset we have—we're going to be an incredible company. There's just no question about it.

AN INFRASTRUCTURE
FOR MOTIVATING OUR PEOPLE

At Umpqua we have an entire infrastructure of rewards, recognition, and engagement programs specifically designed to get our people fired up. The sheer volume and variety of these programs help us ensure that every associate has the opportunity to participate in the success of the organization in some way, however large or small his or her contribution might be.

Here are a few of those programs:

- *Brag Box*. Associates can submit a story of excellence about other associates through the Brag Box on the *Insider*, Umpqua's intranet. Brags are about those who take that additional step to provide an exceptional customer experience. Each month, Brags are selected to receive fifty dollars and special recognition on the *Insider*.

- *Retail Return on Quality (ROQ)*. ROQ is designed to measure individual store progress in a variety of service quality and sales measurements. Customer deposit account retention, new account surveys, Your Opinion Counts surveys, and the number of new deposit and loan accounts per full-time-equivalent employee are included in the current components. Every month, a ranking of store ROQ performance culminates in the top-performing store team being recognized for its outstanding achievement. The highly coveted traveling crystal trophy is presented to the first-place store by senior management, and it is proudly displayed.

- *Department ROQ.* At Umpqua Bank, our focus is on delivering phenomenal customer service—not only for our external customers but internally for other associates and teams. To reinforce this expectation, departments and stores throughout the bank rate each department's internal customer service through an online survey process. A traveling crystal trophy is awarded to the highest-ranking department.

- *Spirit of Excellence awards.* These awards are presented to associates who do extraordinary things for both customers and other associates. They pay attention to the details and surprise and delight others. Award recipients are selected monthly from peer nominations. Winners receive one hundred dollars, a plaque, and an extra day of paid vacation.

- *Team Recognition Fund.* Every store and department has a Team Recognition Fund. Each quarter, the team receives funds per associate (as recorded in the last month of the quarter end). All associates are empowered to use these funds, without supervisor approval, for recognition of other associates.

- *Culture Champion awards.* New to Umpqua's rewards and recognition programs, the Culture Champion awards are in place in some individual business units and managed by their respective executives. Winners are selected based on the department's criteria of cultural excellence.

- *WGBU certification programs.* The World's Greatest Bank University offers certification programs in various functional areas of the bank. On completion of the programs, associates are recognized for their accomplishments with *Insider* announcements, certificates of achievement, graduation ceremonies, recognition luncheons, and more.

- *Years of service awards.* Recognition for years of service is awarded at landmark anniversaries. Each honoree is presented with a gift box including a personalized plaque and gift catalogue. Associates select and order a gift from the catalogue to commemorate their anniversary.

- *Celebration of Excellence.* The Celebration of Excellence recognizes outstanding individual and team performance for the year. Much like the Academy Awards, this gala event's main focus is to celebrate individual and team accomplishments for the year. While many awards are subject to change, here are some that have been presented in the past: Rookie of the Year, Loan Officer of the Year, Store Associate of the Year, Department of the Year, Store Manager of the Year, Store of the Year, and Connect Volunteer of the Year.

- *Annual Chairman's and President's Award.* These two awards are the top honors presented at the Celebration of Excellence each year. The associates who receive these awards exemplify Umpqua's core values, demonstrating an exceptional commitment to providing the highest caliber of customer service. This award includes seven days for two in Hawaii, fifteen hundred dollars in spending cash, and a week's paid time off to enjoy it.

Inspiring, rewarding, and recognizing your people are some of the most important tools you as a leader can wield. Practice these skills, and you will be rewarded with a workforce that is motivated, engaged, and genuinely happy to report to work every day of the week.

FOR REFLECTION

- What do you do to motivate and inspire your employees?

- What do you do that turns them sour on their jobs and their company?

- What are the key components of your company's rewards and recognition infrastructure?

- Do you make a point of personally thanking employees for a job well done? Why or why not?

10

Leverage
Your Assets

Leverage your brand. You shouldn't let two guys in a garage
eat your shorts.
—Guy Kawasaki

Scaling your business is the only option that allows you to continue growing. It demands that you leverage and build on your strengths.

I don't care how large or small your company is, you will always benefit from leverage and scale. In other words, if it takes one hundred dollars to build ten widgets and I can figure out how to build fifty more widgets for that same one hundred dollars, that's something that I want to know. In fact, leverage and scale are so important for businesses in difficult times that they can be essential for a company's very survival. A well-known analyst who spoke at a banking conference I attended in New York City said it this way: "When you look forward in your company, what you need to do is one of these three things: sell it, shut it, or scale it."

And while I personally think those are harsh words, in this type of economy he's probably not too far off.

Every leader, every company owner, every CEO should be on a constant quest for leverage and scale. For the first time in my career—because of the state of the economy and because of competitive factors—I believe that size can make a difference. If you're a small company, how do you leverage yourself into a company that's larger or makes products that you can leverage up?

While you're looking for leverage, however, you've got to be willing to quickly let go of investments that aren't bringing you the results you hoped for. Because an investment in your business has money, employee time, and other significant assets attached to it, it can sometimes be difficult for leaders to abandon and move on. And that creates unproductive assets or resources, which can become a serious drag on a company.

The road ahead is a balance. You're always looking for leverage and scale, but at the same time you've got to be able to let go of the investment you've made in an asset when it's not working.

In my experience, many businesspeople have a hard time letting go of assets because they're eternal optimists. They say, "Just give it a little bit more time, and it will work." And they might be right—or not. I'm an optimist by nature, and I'm glad because I think the alternative stinks. But no matter how optimistic you might be, there's a point when some investments aren't going to work out. When that's the case, the best approach is to cut your losses quickly and move on to more promising investments.

LEVERAGING TECHNOLOGY

A lot of people talk about how they leverage technology to the advantage of their businesses. With the price of much technology as low as it currently is, almost anyone can get what they need no matter what type of company they're running. I take for granted that technology will make things run better, faster, and quicker in my company. But what I'm really interested in when it comes to leveraging technology is what it adds to my value proposition—in other words, how does it contribute to the customer experience? To me, that's where we can most effectively leverage technology. It creates tremendous value, which we like.

When it comes to leveraging assets, people have to be creative. I was on a discussion panel a few years ago with four other bankers representing banks smaller than Umpqua. Each of us on the panel was asked to respond to this question: "In what area of lending are you going to grow this next year?" Now keep in mind that this was during the heart of the recession, 2009 or 2010, and lending was still tight. The moderator worked his way down the row of bankers on the panel, and everybody said they were going to increase their commercial and industrial (C&I) loans—their business loans. When the moderator got to me, I had a different answer.

"Well," I said. "First, yes, like the other four banks on this panel, we are going to grow our C&I lending because we're adding incremental resources to ensure we succeed. So if my friends on the panel today believe they're going to grow their C&I portfolio faster than they have before without adding incremental resources as well, well, I wish them luck." I wasn't very popular when I said that.

I said it in a nice way, but the message was the same: the chances of these other banks growing their C&I loans was low unless they were prepared to invest in the incremental resources required to get the job done. This goes back to when you're building leverage, you've got to know exactly when to invest to have the greatest impact. The trick is timing.

My point was that if these other bankers thought they were suddenly going to grow increased C&I lending in the next year just because they said that they would, I'm afraid they may have been drinking some sort of funny Kool-Aid. I'm going to guess that the people working for these other banks were already working their fannies off. In my opinion, their leaders would have to add people and strengthen their lending infrastructure to produce better results. That's what we did at Umpqua. We scaled up and leveraged the different types of resources and infrastructure changes we needed, giving us the capacity and opportunity to increase our loans.

In this case, some technology leverage was involved, but for the most part it was us going out and hiring away teams of commercial lenders from other banks and markets that we wanted to move into. And what do you think was the biggest draw for us to do that—to get an entire team of people to come from a large, national bank to our small, Oregon-based bank? It was our culture and the value proposition we offer that these men and women were interested in. They had read so much about our culture and value proposition that they were intrigued by it. By no means is our unique culture the right fit for everyone, but it does give us a chance to attract and recruit some really top-notch people.

BUSINESSES ARE MORE EFFICIENT BECAUSE THEY HAVE TO BE TO SURVIVE

The competitive nature of business requires that we constantly become more efficient to compete, survive, expand, improve profits, and thrive in the long run. This is especially true in difficult times, when there's less room to maneuver or make mistakes. As a result, during the course of this most recent economic downturn and the aftermath—which we're still in—companies have aggressively tightened budgets and cut costs. The impact can be seen in the nation's unemployment rate, which I believe is going to take a long time to get back to prerecession levels, if it ever does. This is due to the fact that companies are more efficient now: they don't need as many people to do what they used to do. This, combined with reduced consumer demand, means that companies will be producing less with fewer people than before for at least the foreseeable future.

A lot of companies took advantage of the economic downturn to become more efficient. If it took me ten people to build fifty widgets before the recession, and I've since been able to figure out how to build those same fifty widgets with just six employees—letting go of the four people I no longer needed—when the economy gets better, I'm not going to add those four people back. If I wanted to increase production to eighty widgets to gain market share, I might add one or two employees back, and this then becomes a way to leverage my assets.

If you're not looking to build scale and broaden your span of control (another word for leverage) in today's business environment, I can pretty much guarantee that you're going to have problems. The reason is that in this economy, you need as much room to maneuver as you can find, and you need to figure out how to compete on more than price. And if you think about it, remember that larger businesses, if they've been successful in taking advantage of scale and leverage, can outprice small companies anytime they want, all day long.

I'm not a supporter of growth for the sake of growth, but I do believe that growth can be a very good thing. It needs to be profitable and efficient growth, of course. In the banking industry, smaller community banks make virtually 100 percent of their income from the net interest they generate from their loan portfolios. That doesn't allow much room to maneuver. Larger banks have the ability to add to this by diversifying into other types of revenue-producing activities. giving them more capabilities to improve earnings and leverage their assets. Smaller businesses can't attract the necessary talent and in many cases don't have the capital needed to grow profitably. So, yes, size can be a very good thing in creating leverage—but only if you don't forsake your company just to get larger.

Culture is the greatest asset we possess at Umpqua Bank, and it's also the greatest area of risk because if our company grows and for some reason we forsake our culture, we will have lost what's unique about our business. We would then lose our differentiation, our competitive gap, and our value proposition. Our reputation would go to hell, and our customers would seek other options.

Countless companies have gotten big just for the sake of getting big, and along the way they lost their unique culture. Bureaucracy and process took over, and the company became stagnant and lost its appeal and, with that, whatever competitive gap it had built. There are many companies big and small that have gone out of business because of this reason. As writer Edward Abbey once stated, "Growth for the sake of growth is the ideology of the cancer cell."[1] It can be the death of even the most vigorous and hardy organization.

According to management consultants Graeme Deans and Mary Larson, increasing shareholder value depends on a growth strategy that builds competencies in three distinct areas:

- *Operations:* Becoming the lowest-cost, highest-quality competitor in your industry
- *Organization:* Breaking through growth barriers in your organization and building a growth culture
- *Strategic marketing:* Using the 4Ps of marketing—product, place, price, and promotion—to meet customer needs profitably[2]

Deans and Larson go on to say, "Indeed, absent these competencies, a strategy of growth for its own sake is a trap that is hard to escape. It's also overrated because it's not necessarily attuned to the actual drivers of profitable, long-term growth."[3]

A small business that isn't as efficient as it can be will have difficulty competing. In fact, because small business owners can't compete on price with the large chains, they have to devise a different strategy that will entice customers to shop at their stores. How do you come up with this? I believe it's usually obvious but only after you turn over a lot of rocks.

Here's a hint: you'd better have a better value proposition, a strong reputation, and empowered people. These qualities will help to differentiate your company so you can compete against companies like Walmart on more than just price. If you can't do that you're done.

LEARN TO MAKE 1 + 1 = 4

Growing just for the sake of growth, as some companies do, is not a strategy; in fact, it's a formula for disaster. For example, many companies consider acquisitions to enter new markets or to leverage up assets. It's not a bad strategy unless you're acquiring just to get bigger. But bigger isn't always better. I think that's a weak reason for doing any acquisition.

The key to moving forward with any acquisition is to answer two questions: "What is our strategic rationale for taking this action?" and, "Does it make financial sense?"

The first question, the most difficult hurdle to get over, is the toughest question anyone can ask: "Why?" The answer can't be "just to get bigger"; there has to be a strategic reason. For Umpqua, I want to know the answer to a single question: If we acquire another bank and I apply Umpqua's resources—leveraging all the tools and products we have—can we develop that bank faster than it was growing on its own? If we see growth potential, we're interested in it. If not, we'll pass on the deal.

Not too long ago someone asked me if we would ever consider doing a small transaction because conventional wisdom says they're just as difficult to integrate as a large one and have fewer benefits. My answer surprised them: "It depends on what market it's in." If it's a market with potential and where Umpqua's culture and value proposition would flourish, you bet I'm interested.

The second hurdle—determining the financial metrics of a transaction—is easier. The numbers speak for themselves:

they either add up profitably or they don't. Does the potential profit from the acquisition outweigh the costs? Does it make good financial sense? If the numbers don't support an acquisition, then the strategic rationale better be particularly strong if you're going to proceed any farther down that path.

FOR REFLECTION

- What are you doing to build leverage and scale in your organization?

- In what ways are you leveraging technology? Your financial and human resources?

- In what ways are you making your business more efficient and effective? What are your plans for the future?

- Does your organization pursue growth for growth's sake? If so, what can you do to get off this track?

PART 3

Leading the Way

Capital isn't scarce; vision is.
—Sam Walton

As ubiquitous as the Internet is in our lives today—with our increasing dependence on Internet-enabled e-mail, text and video messaging, streaming video, websites, blogs, and a constantly evolving array of apps—it's hard to imagine that the web has been around for little more than twenty years, and didn't gain widespread use until only about fifteen years ago. Despite this fact, a number of companies have emerged to become leaders in this new industry including Google, Facebook, eBay, and YouTube. Industry leaders come and go, and any company can become a leader if it takes focused action to do so. In this final part, we consider how to develop and maintain a good reputation—both inside and outside the organization—creating buzz, building and maintaining momentum in uncertain times, and practicing incremental evolution.

11

Reputation Counts

It takes 20 years to build a reputation and five minutes to ruin it. If you think about that, you'll do things differently.
—Warren Buffett

Every business depends on its reputation—the social capital it has earned by doing the right thing for its people and their customers and community. Reputation is a reflection of a company's values and how consistently its people adhere to them. A good reputation can carry you far, even in the worst of times. However, it's not easy to build a good reputation; it takes constant and genuine attention to the details, executing the basics well, and consistently delighting customers.

At Umpqua, our four core values are absolute integrity, extraordinary service, innovative delivery, and a strong sense of community as we expand our footprint throughout the nation. Adhering to these core values creates a system of automatic deposits of social capital into our reputation bank. When we fail to live our values, a portion of the social capital we've been accumulating disintegrates and is lost. And as anyone who has lost the trust of a customer knows, social capital that has been lost can be extremely difficult to recover.

OCCUPY UMPQUA

While I have long known that an organization's reputation is an extremely powerful force, this truth was made particularly clear to me when, in the middle of the recent financial crisis, we were faced with an unexpected challenge.

In 2011 Occupy Wall Street became a presence in many large American cities. The organization came into being on September 17 in Zuccotti Park in Manhattan's Financial District, and quickly spread to more than one hundred cities across the country. The reasons for the emergence of the movement can be traced to a variety of grievances, including the widening income gap between rich and poor in the United States, President Obama's perceived failure to hold the financial industry accountable for the 2008 economic crisis that people believed it had in many ways created, and a belief that politics had been taken over by moneyed interests.[1]

The Occupy group in Portland, Oregon, held its first protest march on October 6, 2011. As part of its activities, Occupy Portland planned a day when the group's supporters would occupy Portland banks. I believe that many of the people who belonged to the Occupy Portland organization were decent people who had good motives. But a faction of anarchists had infiltrated the group and was pushing a more radical agenda.

The Occupy Portland website provided information about upcoming protests, marches, and other Occupy events, and we kept an eye on it to monitor the planned action against

Portland banks. As the day drew closer, the affected banks were announced there, and I wasn't surprised to see Wells Fargo, Bank of America, and other large, nationwide banks on the list. We really weren't worried that we would become a target because, compared to those giants, we are a small bank that has deep roots in our communities. We definitely weren't Wall Street.

My bubble was soon burst.

One day someone dropped by my office and said, "Hey, Ray, I just wanted to let you know we were monitoring the Occupy Portland web page and Umpqua's name showed up on it. They're going to march on Umpqua."

"What are you talking about?" I asked. "Are you sure?"

The associate showed me the Occupy Portland web page, and sure enough, the plan was to march on Umpqua Bank. I knew this wouldn't be good for the bank, our associates, or our customers.

A few days later, I asked Eve Callahan, who runs our corporate communications and public relations division, to do me a favor. I said, "I want you to contact Occupy Portland—I want to talk with them."

Eve looked at me as if I'd lost my mind.

"There's a risk in talking with them, Ray."

"I know, Eve," I replied. "But I want to talk with them. Please get ahold of the organization's leadership and set it up. I want to clear the air."

So the leaders of Occupy Portland agreed to meet with us the day before they were set to march on Portland's banks. Everyone—believe me, *everyone*—advised me not to do this. But I was convinced that if I made our case, I might be able to avert this train wreck.

Two polite, articulate young women met us at the Umpqua office at the appointed hour. I thanked them for meeting with me, and then I said, "We're not recording this meeting. This is an opportunity for you to ask me questions and perhaps for me to explain to you what's going on here at Umpqua—what kind of bank we are, what kind of people we are, and what we do for the Portland community."

And they did have questions.

"You received TARP money," began one of the women, "and you never paid it back. Why not?"

"We paid that back two years ago," I explained.

"Oh. You did?" the woman asked.

"Yes we did," I confirmed.

"Oh, okay—I didn't realize that. Here's another question for you. The chairman of your board runs a forest products company. We don't like that."

"You're right," I said, "but what has that got to do with me?"

"Well," the Occupy Portland leader continued, "he's on your board."

"I understand that," I replied, "but help me understand exactly what the problem is. Have you ever met our chairman? He's a great guy. You should introduce yourself to him. I think you'd really like him."

"Well . . ."

I continued. "Now, in what ways do you think I influence his business?"

"What do you mean?" asked the woman.

"I'm not on his board, I'm not his CEO," I explained. "I don't influence his business. I can't tell him what he should or shouldn't be doing."

"Yes, I know that," replied the Occupy Portland leader, "but he's still on your board."

"Okay," I continued, "but let me ask you this: When are you planning to march on the Boys & Girls Club of Oregon? When are you planning to march on the Relief Nursery, which helps underprivileged kids in danger of domestic abuse?"

"What are you talking about?" demanded the Occupy women in unison.

"He's on *their* boards too," I said. "When are you going to march on those organizations because a member of *their* boards—a man who's helping people who have some very serious challenges in their lives—runs a company you don't like?"

The Occupy Portland leaders hadn't thought about that.

After a few more rounds of questions and answers, we wrapped up our conversation and thanked one another for the opportunity to present our respective views in a civil and productive way. And three days later, when Occupy Portland marched on the big banks—the Bank of Americas and the Wells Fargos and all the rest—they didn't march on Umpqua Bank. Now I don't know if that had anything to do with our conversation, but I do know this much: being open and willing to have open communications, a willingness to talk, and a reputation for transparency helped us immensely.

But it didn't end there.

The fact that we were actually willing to meet with the Occupy Portland folks when the larger banks weren't improved our already strong reputation within the community. It made a very large deposit into our social capital bank, one that still earns us interest today.

When you've earned a reputation for being transparent and doing the right thing, the public will give you the benefit of the doubt. And this can make a huge difference in uncertain times.

NO CHIPPED PAINT

In my quest to keep Umpqua a step or two (or three) ahead of our competitors, I study all kinds of companies in a variety of industries—from Starbucks to Disney, and from the Ritz-Carlton to Nordstrom. One thing I've found is that these high-performing companies have several things in common no matter what they sell or what they do.

Perhaps first and foremost among the traits that these companies share is they have extremely high standards and absolutely will not compromise on their high standards.

If you've been to Disneyland or Walt Disney World, you know that the freshly popped popcorn sold throughout the parks is one of their best-selling products. Some people, believe it or not, consider eating Disney's theme park popcorn one of the highlights of their visit. But while many of the parks' guests are enjoying this treat, I dare you to find a stray kernel on the ground. Chances are you won't, at least not for long, because they're picked up immediately by a massive crew of human street sweepers who swarm the parks from opening to closing. The discipline of the company and its people to maintain their standards is incredible.

But I suppose I shouldn't be surprised. Walt Disney's famous vision for this new kind of amusement park that became Disneyland in 1955 was developed years earlier when he was on a trip to a Los Angeles–area amusement park and observed a dilapidated carousel covered in cracked and chipped paint with horses that were broken and frozen in place. These seven words: "No chipped paint. All the horses jump," became Disney's vision for his amusement park of the future. In other words, everything within the theme park would be maintained in pristine condition, and it would work the way it was supposed to.

Each night when the maintenance staff takes control of the park after closing—and before turning the park back over to the ride operators and shopkeepers the next morning— they've got to make sure there's no chipped paint and that things are put back together the way they should.

There are plenty of companies that do incredibly good things—wonderful things, in fact. You'll find these companies in every industry, and in every business market—not just your own. Study them. Learn from their successes. Understand how they recover from mistakes. Explore their core values and cultures.

When I give talks to other bankers, I tell them that if they're looking to get ahead and if they're looking for a wild and crazy idea that might make a difference in these tough times, then take the time to study high-performing companies in a nonbanking industry. Study Disney, Nordstrom, Starbucks, and Apple. Pick a company you admire that's beating the pants off its competition and likes to talk about it. You can bet that their leaders are proud of their success and will be happy to tell you what they're doing since you don't compete with them. So go ask. Then take whatever ideas you learn from them back to your company.

I don't care if you sell insurance or cheeseburgers or widgets or whatever else. The lessons you'll learn from these top-shelf companies are applicable to any industry. Take those lessons back to your office and apply heat to them, bend them, sand and paint them, and then morph them into something that you can use. While you're working on that, keep in mind that your competition doesn't think that way.

If you're in the insurance business, you've got a management or marketing consultant telling you exactly the same thing he's told fifty other insurance companies before yours. As a result, there's no way to differentiate yourself from the pack. By looking outside your industry for ideas, you'll realize that there are as many ways to succeed in business as there are successful businesses, and each has valuable lessons from which we can learn and gain in our own operations.

RIPPLES ON A POND

Every year since 2007, *Forbes* magazine has put Umpqua Bank on its annual list of the Top 100 companies to work for in the United States. For eight years in a row, we've been named the most admired financial services organization in Oregon.

People ask me, "Why do you care about these honors? What do they add to your bottom line?" On the surface they might not appear to add anything directly to our bottom line, but they add to the reputation of Umpqua within our industry and the communities in which we operate. They boost the morale of our people, and that positive energy is reflected back to our clients and our customers. They attract the kind of people we want working for us—people who want to give the best of what they have to give to our customers and to one another.

In tough times, if you have good people capable of doing great work, good leadership capable of communicating effectively, and a strong, well-respected reputation, you're going to make it. You've got everything you need to thrive in even the most uncertain of times.

FOR REFLECTION

- What sort of reputation does your organization have? Among customers? Employees? Your community? Your industry?

- What do you do to build social capital for your business?

- In what ways is your business losing social capital? What are you doing about it?

12

Create Buzz
(But Manage Crisis)

Today brands are everything, and all kinds of products
and services—from accounting firms to sneaker makers to
restaurants—are figuring out how to transcend the narrow
boundaries of their categories and become a brand
surrounded by a Tommy Hilfiger–like buzz.
—Tom Peters

Buzz and word-of-mouth are two of the most effective
ways of getting the word out about your products and
services. Both depend on genuine enthusiasm and interest on
the part of consumers and can light a fire, creating interest and
loyalty for a company's brand and products that's long-lasting
and contagious. Buzz can be both positive and negative. Get
your positive messages out there consistently to build interest
in your brand and products, and be on the lookout for and
neutralize negative buzz as quickly as possible.

It's no longer enough to just have a marketing plan for your
company. In today's fast-changing world of communications,
how we interact with our current and potential customers is

critical. Social media allows companies to interact with and engage customers in new and powerful ways. They make it possible to both listen and speak. In this chapter, we explore how companies can use social media and other vehicles to build relationships and reinforce their reputations in good or difficult economic times.

IN TODAY'S NOISY WORLD, BUZZ IS CRITICAL

Go to any business school, and you'll be taught about the importance of marketing and promoting your company, your brand, and your products and services. And when you dig in a bit deeper, you'll learn that advertising is an important part of the marketing mix—the different approaches that an organization takes in marketing and promotion. While advertising can be an important part of any company's strategy, I believe that before you start booking ads, it's important to first understand the answers to two questions: "What kind of advertising do you need?" and, "When and where can you get the biggest bang for your buck?"

Within the banking industry, our products are for the most part commodities. Every bank has checking accounts, every bank has loans, and every bank will accept your deposits and cash your checks. They all do the same thing. Bank products may come in different colors and may offer slightly different rates, but there's no amazing product in banking that separates one bank from another. And even if one came about, everybody else would quickly copy it.

So how do you advertise that?

In fact, when the larger banks advertise their products and services, they're also advertising for *my* products and services, and for those of every other bank, large, small, or in between. If, for example, Bank of America spends a few million dollars to advertise the virtues of its mobile banking program, it's advertising for me and all other banks because customers assume that every bank offers mobile banking. I realize that advertising is an effective tool to build brand awareness, and perhaps in many industries it's where a marketing budget should be focused. However, for promoting a commodity product like banking, it's often a waste of scarce marketing dollars. The exception is when you have a unique service or product like Apple's iPhone, where advertising helps build a company's competitive gap.

There's so much noise in the world today—we're all constantly being bombarded by messages from the media, from advertisers, from our online friends, and much more—that a lot of advertising simply gets lost. As a result, you've got to ask yourself what you're trying to do with your advertising, because it's not inexpensive—especially for a small business.

I've made the comment publicly that I believe bank advertising is dead, and I have to admit that I get some funny looks when I say that. What I mean is that there are plenty of ads that banks run on television showing warm scenes of kids hugging their grandparents, with the tagline, "Come down and open a checking account at such and such bank." How many people do you think actually say after seeing one of these ads, "Let's run down to the bank and open up a checking account!" I think it's fair to say that it happens very rarely, if at all. Sure—some brand awareness might come out of them, but that's about it.

For most people, when it comes to where they decide to take their banking business, it's all about interest rates or convenience—which bank is located close by and which bank offers the highest interest rates on deposits and the lowest rates on consumer and commercial loans and mortgages. So if I put a very attractive savings account interest rate in the paper that's way above the competition, I'm going to get more business than I know what to do with. By succumbing to this tactic, however, I'm agreeing to compete with price or rates—to reinforce my position as a commodity. Unless you're a big-box retailer where this is part of your value proposition, you've just put your company in a death spiral that you'll be hard-pressed to escape. You can't compete on price alone; it isn't a sustainable strategy.

Becoming a commodity isn't a recipe for long-term success in banking or in any other industry or business. I'm much more interested in creating real value for our customers and then building buzz about our bank.

We started using buzz in our own marketing well before social media came on the scene. What I mean by *buzz* is creating word-of-mouth. At Umpqua, our company is built around creating extraordinary customer experiences that inspire buzz and word-of-mouth from our customers every day. Our associates are trained to go above and beyond to serve their customers. And we empower them to go out in public to create excitement in unexpected ways—we call them random acts of kindness. These random acts can include anything from surprising a group by paying for their lunch or dinner, to giving flowers or picking up the tab for a line of people waiting to order coffee. This creates buzz—people talk about the bank and our great associates, and word spreads through family, friends, and work associates.

RUMORS START FAST (AND BAD NEWS SPREADS FASTER)

We also teach our associates that if things go wrong during the course of a client transaction, they're empowered to do whatever they have to do so the client either leaves our store or hangs up the phone satisfied—not frustrated or angry. We want to turn what could be a negative situation into a positive one because negative customer situations can easily mushroom. The resulting negative buzz can be extremely destructive to a business, so we do our best to identify and resolve any problems while constantly seeking opportunities to generate positive buzz about Umpqua Bank in both traditional (television, radio, newspapers) and social media outlets.

Now, with the reach of social media, negative buzz has the possibility and capability to be much more powerful than positive buzz. One reason word-of-mouth is so successful is that people like to tell others about their experiences, both good and bad. We've all heard that people will tell ten friends about a good or bad experience they've had, and those ten will tell ten others, and so forth. Because of the power of social media, they can now post their experience on Facebook or Twitter or Yelp, multiplying their reach many times over.

Good reports on social media can be terrific and help new customers find your business. Bad news can also take off and in some cases can prove to be the kiss of death for a business that may have made just one unfortunate misstep. While not a literal kiss of death, Netflix (with its 2011 decision to spin off its DVD operation into a new business, Qwikster) and Bank of America (with its 2012 decision to institute new checking account fees) are two recent examples of where social media forced the companies to change course and make customer-centric decisions.

And don't forget: once bad buzz is out there, it's very hard to undo. Negative buzz is *sticky*.

To ensure we don't get stuck in the web of negative buzz, we have people at Umpqua who are assigned the task of listening. They're constantly monitoring social media for comments about Umpqua Bank in order to respond to the comments as quickly as possible. If we see that a customer had a problem and this bad experience is on, say, Facebook or Twitter, we apologize and encourage that person to give us a call so we can address that problem. And we don't stop there. We also reach out to that customer's local store and have that store manager call him or her personally to address the concern and, when appropriate, send a note or gift as a special thank-you. Because of this responsive, hands-on approach, many of these same customers go right back out on Facebook or Twitter and share the experience: "Wow, you won't believe it, but these guys called me and got this thing fixed. I love them!"

Negative buzz is all around us. Just turn on the TV and you'll see plenty of it; do a Google search for information about a specific company, and you'll encounter plenty more. That's a threat to any company, and it's especially unfortunate when the negative buzz is undeserved. The other side of the coin is that if you can create enough positive buzz or word-of-mouth about your business, it can often mitigate the effect of the negative. People expect most businesses to provide customer experiences that aren't particularly noteworthy, so when a restaurant or a store or a bank does something above and beyond the norm, people notice, and the word gets out.

This is exactly what happened when the Winston-Salem, North Carolina–based Krispy Kreme doughnut chain arrived on the West Coast of the United States. Krispy Kreme, founded in 1937, was for most of its history geographically limited to the southeastern United States. Its fans, many of whom had grown up on the sugar-coated, deep-fried doughnuts, were noted for their rabid loyalty and devotion to the company's products. In 1996, after a group of franchisees bought back the company from Beatrice Foods (which had bought Krispy Kreme in 1976 after its founder died), Krispy Kreme began a national expansion.[1] Buoyed by its fanatical customer base, the company became a genuine sensation, generating massive amounts of buzz with each new store opening, proven by the long lines of cars at their drive-up windows all waiting for their freshly made doughnuts.

Unfortunately, Krispy Kreme is also an example of what happens when a company generates negative buzz. The company expanded too quickly, placing its products everywhere it could, including supermarkets, convenience stores, and even casinos. Quality suffered. Not only that, but profit projections were missed, the Securities and Exchange Commission investigated, the company's stock price plunged, shareholders sued, and average weekly sales fell. Krispy Kreme's fans turned on the company in droves, generating huge negative buzz in the process. In 2005 the company's CEO, Scott Livengood, was replaced by Stephen Cooper, who decided to retain his other job just in case—as interim CEO of Enron.[2]

Positive buzz is a significant factor in marketing a business, and building positive buzz goes back to key questions: how you differentiate yourself, how you stand out, and what your culture is built of. If you can build a process within your company, whether you're small, medium, or large, that creates word-of-mouth describing why the way you do business is different and better than your competition's, that's inherently much more powerful and effective than general advertising. People put more credence in the personal testimonies and experiences they hear from their friends or from other "regular" people. It's our hope that the positive buzz we create will lead to these personal testimonies and endorsements from happy customers.

Of course, personal testimonies shared just through advertising are overused and less believable. How many times have you seen a television advertisement for a car dealer that features a happy customer gushing about what a great deal she got and how wonderful the salespeople were? Because every car dealer does that, and it's so commonplace and uneventful, people rarely pay attention to what those happy car customers are saying. This is not buzz. To create positive buzz, you've got to be saying or doing something that inspires others to share it on your behalf.

Forbes contributor Panos Mourdoukoutas detailed how to launch a word-of-mouth and buzz campaign the Apple Way, using Apple Computer as an example of a company that has "grasped the art of WOM and buzz campaigns that have certainly contributed to its phenomenal success." According to Mourdoukoutas, here's how Apple runs its word-of-mouth and buzz marketing campaigns:

1. *Develop a unique product offering*. While Apple's products usually aren't the first in their space (there were numerous

MP3 players before the iPod and plenty of smart phones before the iPhone), they offer distinct advantages over competitive products that make them unique. When the iPhone was released, it beat the pants off the BlackBerry with a larger screen, iTunes integration, maps, calendar, and much more.

2. *Develop the right message.* Apple has mastered the art of merging art and science into an integrated whole, creating great-looking products that can run performance circles around most other products in their categories. When asked to describe the iMac, consumers use such words as *funky*, *glowing*, *extremely friendly*, and *electrifying*. Apple isn't just any old commodity computer maker; it's a powerful branding machine that offers a fantastic value proposition to consumers who happily pay a premium for the company's products.

3. *Target the right group.* Apple's favorite demographic targets are the early adopters, who are constantly on the lookout for the latest-and-greatest product, and the pioneers, who are enamored with anything that is new and exotic. By capturing these two groups, Apple automatically attracts the attention of one more group that is much larger than the early adopters and pioneers: the early majority.

4. *Stir up interest and desire in the product.* Apple's unique ability to merge art and science in its products creates an aura that draws consumers to Apple stores in droves. When Steve Jobs was alive, his product preannouncements, made with great fanfare in specially staged events, consistently created a media frenzy of reporters fighting to get the inside scoop. Even today, the introduction of each new version of the iPhone is enough to create lines of customers who wait for days outside Apple Stores, Best Buys, and

other retailers in hopes of being one of the first people to have an opportunity to buy it.

5. *Turn interest into desire and passion*. The combination of product aura, preannouncements, and limited supply all add up to a powerful blend of catnip for consumers, creating the kind of buzz and word-of-mouth that rockets Apple's products into the mass consumer market, creating huge demand—and sales.

6. *Keep the hype alive*. Not long after a new iPhone, iPod, iPad, or iMac is introduced, the next generation of products is already entering the rumor mill, creating an entirely new round of consumer interest, desire, and passion.[3]

Social media can be a tremendous positive boost for a business, but it can also be a huge negative if it goes unmonitored or if you choose to be unresponsive to people's problems with your organization. Sometimes you've just got to say, "We screwed up, and we're very sorry for that. Come on in; we want to make it right." Turning a negative impression into a positive one can not only correct a bad situation but also create a new fan—someone who will tell their family and friends about what a great company you've got.

YOU ARE BEST AT DELIVERING YOUR MESSAGE

When we say that you are best at delivering your message, it's not just the owner or the leader or the CEO of a business—it's everyone who works for you. If an associate in your company truly believes in what you're trying to do—your products and services, your standards, your ethics, your core values—and is passionate about your organization, think about the power of that. Now multiply that by the number of people in your organization, and you have the power to move mountains.

When people in the field are creating buzz, the buzz that results is much more powerful than the buzz generated by owners or leaders or CEOs. This is because people look at the managers and executives and say, "Well, that's what you're *supposed* to do." And it's true: if you own or lead the business, of course you're going to say it's great. But if I've got ten people who work for me and they're out there saying the same thing, people think, "Wow, these people *really do like* this company." The impression left with the public is much more positive when your own people are saying good things about your company.

Your associates don't become evangelists for your business by accident. If you have the right culture, empower your people, hold them accountable, let them have fun at work, and make them feel good about their jobs, then they're going to want to tell people what a great business they work for.

Guy Kawasaki served for a number of years in the position of chief evangelist at Apple Computer. According to Kawasaki, hiring right is an important part of this process. Says Kawasaki, "Look past the 'perfect' candidate. Ignore the irrelevant. Find the people who believe that your organization can change the world, who use the product. Although I wouldn't have hired me, and still might not today, I was a good candidate for Apple because I was a zealot for the product. Follow your gut: Only hire someone you would enthusiastically run up to if you saw them from a distance. Hire better than yourself."[4]

Owners of businesses who focus on their people and getting them excited about the company they work for can create great waves of success for their organizations. And if the wave is large enough, the media will jump onboard. The media loves stories about companies that are doing something different from the rest of the pack and succeeding at it. Once they pick up on the story, it can take on a life of its own, which can be worth its weight in gold.

CORNY IS (VERY) GOOD

I think corny is good. It stands out. In my experience, people take many of the things in life for granted. For example, I go out to my car, I turn the key in the ignition switch, and I expect the car to start. If it doesn't, I might be late for an important appointment, or I might leave someone stranded at the airport. If I walk into my house and flip on the light switch, I expect the lights to go on. If the lights don't go on, then I won't be able to find my way around the house and might trip on a chair that I'm normally able to avoid when the lights are on. I take it for granted that my car is going to start when I want it to and that my lights are doing to turn on when I flick the switch. These are routine expectations we all have, and most of our waking hours are filled with a long series of such routine expectations that weave the normally uneventful backdrop of our lives.

So when something pops out of that normally uneventful backdrop, people sit up and notice. This is the case when you do something unusual or corny.

One of the first things I did when I came to Umpqua Bank in the mid-1990s was to create some deliberately odd television advertising to help the bank stand out from the crowd and get people to notice us. And it wasn't just corny; it was *really* corny—and funny. The star of these ads was an orangutan that made funny noises while an announcer did a voiceover describing the virtues of banking with Umpqua Bank. We put televisions in the lobbies of the six locations we had at the time and ran those videos nonstop every day. Even now, when I travel to southern Oregon, customers tell me that they still remember those ads with the orangutan. Why? They were unexpected, a surprise and corny!

People also tend to remember the small things. That's why I don't believe in the statement, "Don't sweat the details; just worry about the big stuff." I don't believe that. I think you do need to sweat the details because it's the details that allow the big things to happen.

There are plenty of examples of advertising that's both corny and memorable. Consider the Aflac duck. In case you're not familiar with Aflac (though I'm sure you have seen and remember its television star duck), the company is the nation's largest provider of supplemental insurance to individuals and groups. Much in the same way that I decided to use an orangutan in my early ads for Umpqua Bank, Aflac decided to use a duck in its advertising. That duck is irritating and obnoxious, but it's also so corny and funny that we remember it. In fact, the duck has taken on a life of its own, far beyond the insurance that Aflac sells. The company has created a duck gear store (www.duckgear.com) where you can buy Aflac-branded plush ducks, duck pillows, duck golf club head covers, hats, umbrellas, and much more. And Aflac has sold millions of these items.

POWER OF THE UNEXPECTED

Corny works, and so does the unexpected. If a client had a bad experience with the bank and I as company CEO sent the client some flowers to apologize, that person would certainly appreciate the gesture. But if one of my associates in that store sends that same bouquet of flowers along with a personal note, it results in an even better impression with our customers. Why? Because banking clients don't expect the people in the field to perform random acts of kindness. They expect these gestures to come from the higher-ups. When you empower people at lower levels in the organization to surprise and delight your customers, you can create the power of the unexpected, which in difficult times can help you build the momentum you need to carry you forward into better times.

FOR REFLECTION

- What do you do to create positive buzz and word-of-mouth?

- What do you do to identify and neutralize negative buzz and word-of-mouth?

- What can you do to optimize your buzz and word-of-mouth?

- How do you deliver your message? Are you personally involved? Why or why not?

- How can you unleash the power of being corny and the unexpected?

13

Build Momentum

When you have that window of opportunity called a crisis, move as quickly as you can, get as much done as you can. There's a momentum for change that's very compelling.
—Anne Mulcahy

Momentum may take some time to initiate and build, but once you've got it going, it will carry you and your business far. To build momentum, you've got to know when to hit the gas and when to apply the brakes. You've also got to know when to deploy the supplemental resources, usually people and capital, necessary to accelerate momentum in your organization.

Momentum is powerful. It can be hard to create, and if not caught early, difficult to stop. You can observe momentum just about anywhere, and it can be positive and constructive, or ugly and destructive. A truck without brakes coasting down a steep hill will build momentum—at least until it crashes into a tree or another vehicle. A nasty rumor being spread throughout the workplace can build momentum. An energized sales force convinced they can achieve their quarterly goals can build momentum.

The secret to making momentum a positive force is to harness it and keep it under control, letting it loose when the time is right and can be beneficial.

In business there are hundreds of examples of momentum being developed for the good of a company. You don't have to look far to find them; think of Steve Jobs and the momentum he was able to build for Apple. His own energy propelled Apple to greatness as Apple developed new products regularly that were pertinent, beautiful, and placed into the hands of a passionate sales force. The market share Apple was able to capture was incredible; at one time Apple had the highest market capitalization among public companies in the United States. Although Apple's momentum suffered after Jobs's death, the company's competitors still have a hard time catching up with the power of the Apple brand built under Jobs's tenure. The momentum that Jobs created and Apple benefited from was awe inspiring and a true success story.

KNOW WHEN TO HIT THE GAS, AND WHEN TO SLOW DOWN

One of the secrets of building momentum is timing. When do you hit the gas, and when do you apply the brakes?

At Umpqua we had an opportunity to create momentum at the tail end of the recession, and our timing was critical. As a public company traded on NASDAQ, we regularly make presentations to investors and shareholders about the company's financial performance and prospects for the future. How financial analysts view a public company can make a significant difference in stock value performance as they rate the company's stock. Their ratings of buy, sell, or hold can make a difference on how investors choose to invest.

Depending on the economic or industry issue of the day, analysts tend to place more emphasis on matters that they feel will affect stock performance at that particular time. Before the recession hit, most analysts who followed financial industry stocks were primarily interested in the level and quality of earnings, or earnings per share of a company. Once the recession took hold, everything changed, and analyst perspectives changed quickly. Sentiments of financial analysts turned sharply away from earnings to this question: "Do you have enough capital and liquidity to survive this economic crisis?"

At Umpqua our earnings before the recession were always strong, and our capital and liquidity levels after the recession have always been viewed as extremely healthy. There's no issue there.

However, the story continues.

Once earnings and capital were addressed, it didn't take long for a new concern to emerge among analysts: "How bad are your loan losses going to be during this period, and how strong is your loan portfolio?"

As we now know, all banks suffered from loan losses during the recession. So the real question was this: "How fast can you work your way through this mess while you minimize your losses?" At Umpqua, we worked our tails off over the next couple of years before we saw light at the end of the tunnel on the credit quality issue. But we did see the light, and, no, it was not a train bearing down on us out of a tunnel! We also realized that since Wall Street is fickle at best, we could anticipate the next questions we would soon be quizzed on: "Can you lead your business to growth in this environment?" and "Let's talk about the level and quality of your earnings." We were headed right back where we started.

The moment we saw the light on credit quality—and even though we still had work to do in this area—we got busy, busy, busy building momentum. We wanted to be able to show growth in our business before we were asked. The question was how best to make this happen. Remember that no one was paying much attention to earnings as they concentrated on balance sheet issues.

So we invested: We ramped up investments in our infrastructure and expanded our loan delivery system into new markets. We completed a couple of acquisitions, invested in non-interest-income-producing departments, and attracted new talent to the company—people who could add incremental growth.

We made all of these decisions, and many more, for one reason: to build momentum. We were finally playing offense instead of defense and taking control of our own destiny. It felt good. Over the next eight quarters, Umpqua reported strong new-loan growth, proving that, yes, our company could grow in a depressed economy and we had the numbers to prove it.

We knew it was time to hit the gas and start building our momentum when we saw clear signs that we were emerging from the recession. One aspect of momentum to keep in mind is that it often takes time to build; it doesn't just happen overnight. It's sort of like when I was a kid and my brother and I had a siren we liked to play with. It was hard to turn at first, but once we got the flywheel inside the siren turning, the easier it was to turn, and, man, did that thing get loud. Momentum can also be fun.

Unfortunately, momentum can also work against you if you let it. When unattended and ignored, negative events can take on a life of their own, build momentum, and be difficult to stop, just like that truck careening down the hill with no brakes. You can also unintentionally add momentum to bad things, and in doing so make them that much harder to stop or turn positive. If momentum is being built around a decision that could bode poorly for you or your company, get your foot off the gas and stop that decision as early and as quickly as you can. You have to know when to pull back!

WITH UNCERTAIN TIMES COME GREAT OPPORTUNITIES

Effective leaders always look beyond the present. They look into next week or even a year or more ahead. They keep their eyes on the horizon, searching for the next opportunity, the next revolution. Opportunities can show up at any time, during good times and bad, because good times don't own the market on opportunities.

When the recession was creating havoc with the financial industry, many banks failed. Customer deposits are insured by the Federal Deposit Insurance Corporation (FDIC), and like any other insurance company, it had a strong desire to minimize any losses it might sustain through bank failures. One strategy the FDIC pursued to minimize its losses was to have strong, healthy banks take over the seriously weak banks under terms that were good for both the FDIC and the healthy bank. Although regulators recognized that Umpqua was a strong institution, we nevertheless had issues created by the recession to work out.

However, opportunity knocked, as they say, and Umpqua bid on and was successful in taking over four failed banks during this period. Three of these banks were in the state of Washington and one was in Reno, Nevada. All welcomed Umpqua when we arrived, and for good reason. By stepping in, we preserved community banking in their towns and cities, providing the long-term stability, convenience, and resources of a larger institution but maintaining the local commitment and engagement of a smaller bank. But perhaps just as important, our new associates in the acquired banks have enthusiastically embraced Umpqua and our unique culture. It's truly a win-win for everyone.

By keeping ourselves open to and watching for opportunities during tough economic times, we both helped out the FDIC and benefited ourselves by way of these financially lucrative transactions. We were able to expand into new markets that have proven to be success stories for us and for our new customers, who now have stable banks in their communities.

Chuck Robinson, who served as U.S. deputy secretary of state and was a long-time member of Nike's board of directors, is a big believer in the idea that you've got to leverage every possible advantage you can in your effort to beat the competition. According to Chuck, tilting the playing field in his favor brought him tremendous success in business. Says Robinson,

> Everybody says, "Give me a level playing field to compete on." I say, "How stupid can you be?" The game is to tilt the playing field in your favor. You tilt the playing field by anticipating the flow of history and positioning yourself to take advantage of things that are going to develop on ahead. If you make a decision based on all the facts you know today, you're bound to be wrong because the gestation period for taking an idea to commercial exploitation can be one year or five years or even ten years. So if you make a decision based on what the conditions are today,

you're bound to be wrong. You have to ask yourself, "What are the factors that are bringing about change, and where is that going to lead three years from now, or five years from now? What do I need to do today to be positioned to take advantage when all this comes together?"[1]

There are always opportunities to be acted on and leveraged, even in the most uncertain times. Your job as a leader is to be alert to them when they arrive and then to have the self-confidence and wherewithal to grab them and convert them into something good for your organization. Opportunities can and often do arrive when you least expect them, so keep your eye on the horizon and your ear to the ground.

BRING IN INCREMENTAL RESOURCES TO BUILD MOMENTUM

Investing in incremental resources—particularly in people—can accelerate positive momentum for an organization. I always tend to give people the benefit of the doubt unless they let me down, and then it's hard to earn back my trust. During uncertain times, I believe that management is truly trying not to screw things up. People work as hard as they can to make progress for their companies. But some managers do try to wring as much out of their employees as they can and are often disappointed when these efforts don't substantially move the needle. Others practice the proverbial definition of insanity, where they ask their people to do the same thing over and over again and yet expect better results.

If people are already running as fast as they humanly can, how can you expect them to produce more? You can squeeze only so much out of people before you start affecting their ability to do their jobs well. In the worst case, they either burn out or leave the company. Not very productive.

One of the ways to prevent this, and to build momentum at the same time, is to know when to add incremental resources. In our case, we wanted to increase our loans and felt that due to the economic circumstances, we could not expect our people to work any harder or produce stronger growth. So again we invested, this time in new loan professionals in new markets. Moving into new markets was a key part of our strategy because we felt that in some markets we already were in, more people would actually result in diminishing returns. In other words, our incremental growth in current markets would be small; however, the same new resources in new markets could generate substantial new growth. We saw that our opportunity for growth was greater in new markets, so we took advantage of it and created momentum for new loan growth we otherwise would not have achieved.

Leadership is about knowing when to add incremental resources. By definition, incremental resources can add incremental revenues and growth. And during uncertain times, growth is a very good thing. But incremental resources can also add one more thing: momentum. There's not a single organization I'm aware of that wouldn't benefit from gaining momentum—in its marketing and buzz, revenue and sales, growth of market share, and bottom line.

Be aware of your organization's momentum in the marketplace and constantly seek out new ways to maintain or increase it. In my experience, adding incremental resources is one of the best ways to build momentum, so be sure to explore the possibilities for using this approach to taking your organization to the next level.

FOR REFLECTION

- How do you build momentum in your organization? What power does it hold?

- What are your competitors doing to build momentum, and what are you doing to keep up or overtake them?

- When do you hit the gas, and when do you hit the brakes?

- What unique opportunities are available to your business right now, during these uncertain times? What are you going to do to convert them into new business?

- How can adding incremental resources take your business to another level?

14

Practice Incremental Evolution

Extinction is the rule. Survival is the exception.
—Carl Sagan

Some would say that businesses are like plants: if they're not growing, they're dying. While businesses and plants in reality have little or nothing in common with one another, it's true that companies have to grow and change to remain vital and strong. In his book *Leading the Revolution*, Gary Hamel writes about the importance of establishing and nurturing a competitive gap.[1] Competitive gaps are innovations that companies create to separate themselves from their competitors.

The moment you create a competitive gap, you've constantly got to find ways to maintain it. This requires either creating new quantum leaps that dramatically widen the gap or practicing incremental evolution, which maintains your competitive gap through smaller changes and improvements to your products, your selling proposition, and your delivery vehicles. Quantum leaps are rare, so incremental evolution is the name of the game.

When we established our first concept store in Roseburg, Oregon, in 1996, we opened up a competitive gap for our company that revolved around a unique product delivery system that we call "bank stores." The success of our store design created a tangible competitive advantage for Umpqua, which almost overnight created a huge separation between us and the rest of our competition. Customers who were used to shopping banks based on interest rates or monthly fees (or the lack thereof) were attracted to our value proposition—one that offered the sights, smells, and amenities of a retail experience combined with competitive interest rates and a one-of-a-kind customer service experience. The moment prospective customers stepped into one of our stores, they knew they were in for a unique banking experience.

However, if all we did was bring a retail experience to banking, our advantage might not have lasted long at all, and our competitive gap could have quickly closed. To succeed in the long run, we had to execute the basics well: we had to be the world's greatest bankers working for the World's Greatest Bank. Combining our innovative banking stores with associates who really care about their customers and do their jobs exceedingly well has made it extremely hard for competitors to close the gap—if they even try.

Differentiation is not a new concept in business; every company is looking for ways to stand out from the competition and create competitive gaps. However, these gaps aren't always easy to find, and they can be even more difficult to develop and sustain.

As tough as competitive gaps are to create most of the time, every now and then one lands in your lap or is staring you right in the face. For Umpqua, it wasn't about technology and more branch locations. It was all about how we delivered our products and services. And because the approach we decided to pursue was so unique—and to some naysayers, even corny—it created a significant competitive gap for us. This built our reputation, which helped build our unique Umpqua Bank culture, which created our value proposition. Momentum! These intangibles were stepping-stones that enabled us to take advantage of when things were good and to rely and depend on when times became challenging.

SUSTAINING A COMPETITIVE GAP

While a competitive gap is wonderful to have—essential, in fact, for long-term growth and success—it can also be a burden, since you have to constantly manage, reinforce, and see that it evolves. Fail to do that, and you can lose it. As Hamel points out, competitive gaps can lose their appeal, they can be copied, they can get worn out, and over some period of time they will erode if you don't constantly repolish them.

Our competitive gap came from the unique delivery system we created in the banking industry—our stores—that helped us get out in front of our competition, gave our customers a clear differentiated choice, and, as it turned out, became a stimulant to many other institutions within the banking industry. It was a quantum leap for us that continues to be successful.

As we expected, other banks have tried to close the gap we created by copying our approach. Our challenge now is the same as any other company that has created a competitive gap: to sustain it. In my experience, there are two ways to accomplish this.

The first approach is to create new quantum leaps of change that are specifically designed to create and develop entirely new aspects of the competitive gap you've already built. The second approach, which I believe is usually the direction most companies take, is to make incrementally smaller changes on a regular basis that breathe new life into your strategy.

It should be no surprise that everyone is looking for the quantum leap of change that will launch their company far ahead of their competition. The reason is that quantum leaps are significant game changers that can be meaningful and long lasting. Think of IBM's original personal computer (which brought small desktop computers first to businesses, then to individuals worldwide), the Xerox copier (which made photostats, carbon paper, and mimeograph machines obsolete), and the Apple iPod and iPhone (which took the world of portable music players and smart phones by storm). Each of these products represented quantum leaps of change in their respective industries, and each gave their companies a huge competitive gap that lasted for years. In each case, they weren't the first such product in their industries, but they were the best. They captured the public's attention—and their dollars. But finding something new and innovative in your industry that constitutes a quantum leap is not easy, and many companies never do it.

Maintaining the competitive gap that results from a significant innovation in a company's products or services is a full-time job; you can't afford to rest on your laurels. If it's that good, people are going to copy it. And if you keep doing the same thing over and over again, people are going to get tired of it. To maintain your competitive gap, you have to constantly tweak your product and service offerings, and you've got to make changes that will keep your customers interested in what you offer while you continue to look for new ways to stay ahead of the competition.

In my experience, one of the best ways to do this is to study industries outside your own.

STUDY INDUSTRIES OUTSIDE YOUR OWN

There's a very good reason that I seldom hire bank consultants: they are going to tell me exactly the same thing they've told ten other banks, and that advice isn't going to be life changing for our company. Instead, I like to hire people from outside the banking industry to help me because they've got different ideas and bring with them an entirely different base of experience. It reminds me of the old advertisement for Apple computers: *Think Different.* When you take a look at your business through the lens of a different industry, you can see a lot of things that you would never otherwise see and come up with new ideas that you can tailor to your own purposes.

One way to practice this is to find a company that's beating their competition soundly and then study it in great depth. What makes it a success? Why can't its competitors respond? What's its secret?

At Umpqua Bank, we've studied a variety of companies outside the banking industry over the years, including Disney, Ritz-Carlton, the Gap, and Nike. In addition, we've talked to the people running and working in these companies about the way they do things and what it is that allows them to routinely beat the pants off the other companies in their industry. To make an idea from a different industry work for us, we'll bring it into our company, talk about it, beat it up, change a few things here, modify a few things there, and then give it a try in one of our stores.

If it works, we keep it. Otherwise we toss it.

What's particularly interesting to me about the concept of studying industries outside our own is that for the most part, our competitors aren't doing what we're doing. In the case of the banking industry, most banks are busy studying and comparing themselves to other banks—not with businesses in completely different industries. I believe this is true for most businesses. Few look outside their own industries for ideas, either because they don't see the value of doing this, or they think the best answers are in their own industries, or they simply don't even think about it—it's not within the boundaries of their paradigm.

If I owned a car dealership, I could very well hire an efficiency expert and have that person come in to help me figure out ways to improve the way we handle car repairs. That could certainly be very useful, and it might make my business somewhat better. But why not also consider bringing in someone from the hospitality industry who could help me improve the way I handle customers while they are waiting for their cars to be serviced?

Ten years ago, the customer waiting room in most car dealerships in the United States was a pretty dreary place. The room was usually small and filled with hard plastic chairs with a few car magazines scattered around and a television bolted high up in a corner (usually running at full volume with a channel changer nowhere to be seen). If you wanted something to drink or eat, there was a vending machine around the corner for employees that you were welcome to use too, assuming you brought the proper change. And if you wanted to relax for a while or try to get some work done, forget it. There was nowhere to stretch out and work, and besides, that TV blaring in the corner of the room wasn't exactly conducive to doing anything that might require concentration.

Today, however, it's not uncommon for customer waiting *lounges* in car dealerships to be much larger and stocked with comfortable chairs, desks on which to plant your laptop computer, Wi-Fi, complementary refreshments (coffee, tea, and water), and maybe even freshly baked cookies. And as you find a place to plant your laptop and yourself, there's a good chance that a new car salesperson will wander over to see if you would like any useful information about the dealer's stock of trucks, SUVs, and automobiles and the hot deals that just happen to be going on while your car is in for service.

This is obviously quite a far cry from the car dealership waiting rooms of old. Of course, the dealership still has to execute the basics well—it needs to do a great job fixing your car at a good price—but the best companies in this industry have figured out how to turn what was once a fairly unpleasant experience into one that is, dare I say it, enjoyable.

Most people hate taking their cars to the shop, and little subtleties like this can make a huge difference in the way your business is perceived by customers and whether they tell their friends and relatives about the experience. Studying industries outside your own can go a long way to help you either incrementally change your own value proposition or perhaps even stumble on one of those game-changing quantum leap innovations that could transform your industry—and your company.

EASIER TO DO IN GOOD TIMES THAN IN BAD

There's no question that it's easier to make incremental updates to your company in good times than in bad.

First, in tough times, most business leaders have their attention fully focused on simply surviving, not on making minor tweaks to their business model to build or maintain a competitive gap. And if there are additional costs associated with incremental changes to your value proposition, then they're hard to justify.

Second, when times are good, you naturally have plenty of elbow room to maneuver and can take time out to think of creative, nutty, corny things that will make a difference. When things are difficult, you don't really have the luxury to do this. It's kind of like someone with a parachute who jumps out of a plane at ten thousand feet. At that altitude, the parachutist has time—thirty seconds or more—to maneuver around and enjoy the sights before pulling the ripcord. However, the same person with a parachute who jumps out of a plane at five hundred feet is going to be scrambling to pull the ripcord the moment she clears the airplane. If the parachutist wants to land safely, there will be no time to enjoy the sights on that short trip to the ground. The only thing that parachutist will be looking for is the handle to pull the ripcord that will deploy her parachute.

In business, you've always got to deal with the problems at hand, but when times are good, you have more time to focus on doing the things you *want* to do instead of just the things you *have* to do.

Nevertheless, when times are uncertain, there are ways to give yourself more elbow room. Some things are life-threatening to a business and must be dealt with immediately, regardless of the economic climate or the competitive environment. But if the problems aren't severe, you can have confidence in your people and give them the authority they need to deal with the problems so that you can move on to something else.

Imagine for a moment a small business that's faced with a customer service issue at the same time that the owner knows that she's got to get sales up the next quarter. The owner can get her customer service team together and say, "Okay, you've got to get this fixed; here's your time frame. Now get going and let me know if you have any questions along the way." If the owner has the right people assigned to the task of addressing the customer service issue, then she can turn her attention to doing whatever is necessary to improve sales. By leveraging her people, the small business owner created the elbow room she needed to address the issue while also working on the company's lagging sales.

I tell people that if you're going to apply part-time resources to something that's important, you're going to get part-time results. So when you see things that need to get done that are important to your business, make sure you're applying the resources necessary to get it done. I've watched too many people trying to tackle five or six or seven different projects at once and getting strung out because they can't finish any one of them before something else happens to another one. I'd rather have them get one task done and then come back for the next one. I'll give it to you then, but I want to see progress made first.

FOR REFLECTION

- Does your company have a competitive gap? What is it, and how large is it?

- What are you doing to establish a new competitive gap or develop the one you already have?

- What are the potential benefits to your organization of looking at highly successful businesses in other industry for new ideas? What can you do to make this happen?

Conclusion: Lead On

People want and expect their leaders to lead, and good leaders have the skill and talent to do just that: lead.

We know that if people don't trust or have confidence in their leaders, problems can and will occur. At a minimum, these problems can damage a business's reputation with customers and the public. At their worst, these problems can stop a business dead in its tracks. Nobody said it was going to be easy; in fact, leadership can be downright difficult and frustrating. However, it can also be uplifting and motivating—a source of real inspiration—when practiced effectively.

A leader can be anyone at any level in an organization who's responsible for people: a chief executive officer, a division or department officer, the head of the accounts payable team, and the list goes on. All of these leaders, and others in positions of authority, need one basic skill to lead effectively, and that is to be able to motivate and inspire their people with optimistic passion. Without this essential characteristic, true leadership becomes impossible.

We've all worked with or for an individual who was a true motivator and inspired us to reach for higher ground because we really wanted to get there. This kind of leader quickly earns the trust and confidence of others and ingrains a can-do attitude throughout their team or organization. This leader also will be given the benefit of the doubt when difficulties arise, or when tough love needs to be practiced to get the job done. We've also worked with leaders who simply dictated what they wanted accomplished. These people don't normally last very long.

When you break down the role of leadership to its most basic element, I believe you end up with one word that truly summarizes what a leader deals with day in and day out: *persuasion*. Leadership is the act and art of persuasion. For example, leaders try to get their people to see the value of their mission, motivate people to the next level, encourage fellow associates to reach for higher and more productive goals, and constantly attempt to convince others that there are solutions to even the most difficult and intractable problems. These are just a few of the hundreds of issues a leader deals with on a regular basis. We also know that effective leaders realize that they're not an army of one. They need their people to enthusiastically get behind them and accelerate their business toward the objectives that are of strategic importance to the company, and hence also their people.

In times of uncertainty, leadership is especially vital because you must deal with difficult issues and situations while you also make progress toward goals that will help you navigate your company into calmer waters. In this environment, effective leaders must be nimble and agile, and stay in touch with the latest news and issues affecting the industry in order to make a difference. They also have to keep the bigger picture in perspective to make sure they don't lose the war while winning a battle.

Let's face it: leadership can be overwhelming. And times of uncertainty add another dimension of difficulty. It brings to mind perhaps one of the most difficult questions for any leader to answer: How?

No matter what level you are within your organization, the topics discussed in this book apply to you. The order and priorities you set for each will be your decision in answering the "How?" question. While you formulate your strategy, keep the following in mind. First, doing nothing is simply not an option. Second, don't act just to act; be deliberate and be smart. And third, remember that any leader can make a difference and that small beginnings can lead to big results.

As you lead through uncertainty, make sure you build your own personal foundation to ensure success. I believe this starts with an introspective and honest inventory—first of yourself and then of your organization. Companies regularly evaluate their strengths, weaknesses, opportunities, and threats to make sure they are focused on the right issues. I wonder, however, how many leaders do the same evaluation on themselves. I recommend this as a good starting point.

Finally, ask yourself the following questions: "When you think of your organization, what inspires you?" "What are you passionate about?" Once you answer these questions, you will know the answer to that "How?" question and will be able to establish the right strategies to lead your company through times of uncertainty. The answer is inside each of you. Now go find it.

Notes

Chapter One: The New Normal

1. Ashley Halsey III, "Airport Delays Provide Lesson on Infrastructure, Operations Costs," *Washington Post*, April 27, 2013, http://articles .washingtonpost.com/2013–04–27/local/38857630_1_sequestration-airport-improvement-funds-faa.

2. Robert W. Fairlie, "Kauffman Index of Entrepreneurial Activity, 1996–2012," Ewing Marion Kauffman Foundation (April 2013), http:// www.kauffman.org/uploadedFiles/KIEA_2013_report.pdf.

3. Stu Woo, "Under Fire, Netflix Rewinds DVD Plan," *Wall Street Journal*, October 11, 2011, http://online.wsj.com/article/SB10001424052970203 499704576622674082410578.html.

4. Peter Fuda, "Why Change Efforts Fail," *Peter Fuda and the Alignment Partnership* (2009), 1.

5. John Kotter, "Can You Handle an Exponential Rate of Change?" Forbes blog, http://www.forbes.com/sites/johnkotter/2011/07/19/can-you-handle-an-exponential-rate-of-change/.

6. Paul Polak, "Four Transformative Business Opportunities in Emerging Markets," March 13, 2012, http://blog.paulpolak.com/?p=1645.

7. "Fedex Corp—Early History," May 12, 2013, http://ecommerce.hostip .info/pages/443/Fedex-Corp-EARLY-HISTORY.html.

8. "FedEx Corporation Company Information," May 12, 2013, http://www.hoovers.com/company-information/cs/company-profile.FedEx_Corporation.e6bc953d777db293.html; "History of FedEx Operating Companies," May 12, 2013, http://about.van.fedex.com/fedex-opco-history

9. Steve Friess, "Vegas' Newest Gimmick: ATM That Dispenses Gold," AOLNews, January 8, 2011.

10. Joseph Schumpeter, *Capitalism, Socialism, and Democracy* (New York: Psychology Press, 2003), 207.

Chapter Two: The Truth, Nothing But the Truth

1. Brier Dudley, "More Layoffs at T-Mobile, Engineering This Time," *Seattle Times*, April 3, 2013, http://blogs.seattletimes.com/brierdudley/2013/04/03/more-layoffs-at-t-mobile-engineering-this-time/.

2. Mark Madler, "Merger Prompts First California Layoffs," *San Fernando Valley Business Journal*, March 29, 2013, http://www.sfvbj.com/news/2013/mar/29/merger-prompts-first-california-layoffs/.

3. Rita Schiano, "Fear's Connection to Anxiety," April 16, 2013, http://www.psychologytoday.com/blog/in-the-face-adversity/201304/fears-connection-anxiety.

4. Mick Ukleja and Robert Lorber, *Who Are You and What Do You Want?* (Des Moines, IA: Meredith Books, 2008), 37.

5. B. Kaada, "The Sudden Infant Death Syndrome Induced by 'the Fear Paralysis Reflex'?" *Medical Hypotheses* 22 (1987): 347–356, http://www.ncbi.nlm.nih.gov/pubmed/3647223.

6. "Fear Paralysis Reflex," May 12, 2013, http://www.retainedneonatal-reflexes.com.au/reflexes-explained/reflexes-fear-paralysis-reflex/.

7. "Odwalla, Inc., Company Information," May 12, 2013, http://www.hoovers.com/company-information/cs/company-profile.Odwalla_Inc.fe5d7db057dfbbf3.html.

8. Anni Layne, "How to Make Your Company More Resilient," *Fast Company* (February 28, 2001).

9. Ibid.

10. Ibid.

11. Ibid.

Chapter Three: Problems and the Healing Process

1. Pallavi Gogoi, "No Sign of Shareholder Revolt against Dimon," AP, May 14, 2012, http://bigstory.ap.org/content/no-sign-shareholder-revolt-against-dimon.

Chapter Four: Control and Uncertainty

1. Douglas A. McIntyre, Ashley C. Allen, Samuel Weigley, and Michael B. Sauter, "The Worst Business Decisions of All Time," *Free Republic*, October 17, 2012, http://www.freerepublic.com/focus/f-chat/2946112/posts.

2. Sam Mamudi, "Lehman Folds with Record $613 Billion Debt," *MarketWatch*, September 15, 2008. http://www.marketwatch.com/story/lehman-folds-with-record-613-billion-debt.

3. Erik Klemetti, "Volcano Profile: Mt. Hood," April 24, 2009, http://scienceblogs.com/eruptions/2009/04/24/volcano-profile-mt-hood/.

4. Jean-François Manzoni and Jean-Louis Barsoux, "The Set-Up-to-Fail Syndrome," *Harvard Business Review* (March 1998), 101–113.

Chapter Five: Exercise Your Intuition

1. "Trust Your Gut: Intuitive Decision-Making Based on Expertise May Deliver Better Results Than Analytical Approach," *Science Daily*, December 20, 2012, http://www.sciencedaily.com/releases/2012/12/121220144155.htm/.

2. "In Decision-Making, It Might Be Worth Trusting Your Gut," December 14, 2012, *Science Daily*, http://www.sciencedaily.com/releases/2012/12/121214191243.htm

3. Eugene Sadler-Smith and Erella Shefy, "The Intuitive Executive: Understanding and Applying 'Gut Feel' in Decision-Making," *Academy of Management Executive* 18 (2004): 80–81.

4. A. M. Hayashi, "When to Trust Your Gut," *Harvard Business Review* (February 2001), 59–65.

Chapter Six: Be Really Good at the Basics

1. Lynne Terry, "Health Officials Investigate Norovirus Outbreak at Andina in Portland," *Oregonian*, March 13, 2013.

Chapter Seven: The Value of a Value Proposition

1. Peep Laja, "Useful Value Proposition Examples (and How to Create a Good One)," *Conversational*, February 16, 2012, http://conversionxl .com/value-proposition-examples-how-to-create/.

Chapter Eight: Be Available

1. Frances Hesselbein, *Hesselbein on Leadership* (San Francisco: Jossey-Bass, 2002), xii-xiii.
2. Ibid., xvi.
3. Daniela Yu, Jim Harter, and Sangeeta Agrawai, "U.S. Managers Boast Best Work Engagement" (Washington, DC: Gallup Organization, April 26, 2013).

Chapter Nine: Motivate and Inspire

1. Bob Nelson, *1501 Ways to Reward Employees* (New York: Workman Publishing, 2012), 9.
2. Ibid.
3. Ibid., 3.
4. Ibid., 10.

Chapter Ten: Leverage Your Assets

1. Edward Abbey, *The Journey Home: Some Words in Defense of the American West* (New York: Plume, 1991), 183.
2. Graeme Deans and Mary Larson, "Growth for Growth's Sake: A Recipe for a Potential Disaster," *Organization* (September/October 2008), http://www.iveybusinessjournal.com/topics/the-organization/growth-for-growths-sake-a-recipe-for-a-.potential-disaster#.Ub9YwPZARMg
3. Ibid.

Chapter Eleven: Reputation Counts

1. Max Chafkin, "Revolution Number 99," *Vanity Fair* (February 2012), http://www.vanityfair.com/politics/2012/02/occupy-wall-street-201202.

Chapter Twelve: Create Buzz (But Manage Crisis)

1. Kate O'Sullivan, "Kremed! The Rise and Fall of Krispy Kreme Is a Cautionary Tale of Ambition, Greed, and Inexperience," *CFO* (June 1, 2005), http://www.cfo.com/article.cfm/4007436.

2. Ibid.

3. Panos Mourdoukoutas, "How to Launch a WOM and Buzz Campaign the Apple Way," August 7, 2011, http://www.forbes.com/sites/panos mourdoukoutas/2011/08/07/how-to-launch-a-wom-and-buzz-campaign-the-apple-computer-way/.

4. "The Evangelist's Playbook," *Success*, May 12, 2013, http://www.succcss .com/articles/1112-the-evangelist-s-playbook.

Chapter Thirteen: Build Momentum

1. Peter Isler and Peter Economy, *At the Helm: Business Lessons for Navigating Rough Waters* (New York: Doubleday, 2000), 86.

Chapter Fourteen: Practice Incremental Evolution

1. Gary Hamel, *Leading the Revolution: How to Thrive in Turbulent Times by Making Innovation a Way of Life* (Boston: Harvard Business School Press, 2002).

Acknowledgments

Since the publication of my first book in 2007, *Leading for Growth*, the "normal" that we were all used to in the economy, the housing market, and basically all other facets of our daily lives has changed and perhaps left us forever. The uncertainty that has replaced it has proven to be more than difficult; it's been downright lousy. During this period, we've seen leaders rise to the occasion and show their true mettle, and we've witnessed some who gave up, gave in, or just couldn't play the hand they had been dealt. One thing is certain: over the past five to six years, leadership has never been more needed, wanted, or required. I've been thinking of writing this book for several years, not from the position of being a leadership expert (which I'm not) but from a commonsense point of view that offers leadership characteristics that leaders are and have been aware of and know they must practice to succeed.

I am reminded of these points on a regular basis by the more than twenty-five hundred Umpqua associates who hold me accountable to live up to our own company standards. I acknowledge these terrific people and thank them for giving me the benefit of the doubt and continuing to blow wind in my sails as we together advance a great company. Others at Umpqua who have played an important role in all our successes include our board of directors—leaders in the truest sense of the word: Allyn Ford, Peggy Fowler, Bill Lansing, Bryan Timm, Hilliard Terry, Susan Stevens, Laureen Seeger, Stephen Gambee, Jim Greene, Luis Machuca, Diane Miller, Dudley Slater, and Frank Whittaker. They have tolerated my inconsistencies with grace, and for that I thank them.

I also thank my leadership team—those who deal with my rants and unbridled passion about Umpqua: Barbara Baker, Brad Copeland, Ron Farnsworth, Lani Hayward, Kelly Johnson, Gary Neal, Cort O'Haver, Steve Philpott, and Mark Wardlow. Special thanks go out to Lorelei Brennan, my executive assistant, for being who you are, and to Eve Callahan for being the catalyst to move me to get this book completed. Thanks, Eve, for your ideas, editing, and encouragement.

It goes without saying that without Peter Economy, this book would still be just a good idea. Peter, your sprint to the finish line was incredible. Thank you for your partnership in this project. As some have said, "We did good." I also thank all the people at Jossey-Bass who accommodated our untimely requests, including our editor, Karen Murphy, for showing us the path we needed to follow to bring this book in on time.

And to my family—Aimee, Kyle, Brooke, Jackson (my best friend), and Caroline (I'm thinking of you!)—who unknowingly motivate me every single day. Finally, to Bobbi, who makes all my dreams come true. Without you, nothing would have made sense. ILYTMOTU.

About the Authors

Ray Davis is a pioneer of change in the banking industry, revolutionizing how banks look, feel, sound, and operate. As president and CEO of Umpqua Holdings Corporation, parent company of Umpqua Bank, Davis took a small, regional bank with six locations and developed it into one of the most innovative and dynamic community banks in the United States. He has been recognized in numerous national publications, including the *Wall Street Journal*, *New York Times*, *Fast Company*, *BusinessWeek*, *Business 2.0*, *Newsweek*, and CNBC, and he is the author of *Leading for Growth: How Umpqua Bank Got Cool and Created a Culture of Greatness*. Davis has been recognized as one of high finance's twenty-five most influential people by *U.S. Banker Magazine*. Davis lives with his wife in Portland, Oregon. For more information, please visit www.umpquabank.com.

* * *

Peter Economy is associate editor of *Leader to Leader*, the award-winning magazine of the Frances Hesselbein Leadership Institute. He is also the best-selling author, coauthor, or ghostwriter of more than sixty books, including *The SAIC Solution: How We Built an $8 Billion Employee-Owned Technology Company*; *Lessons from the Edge: Survival Skills for Starting and Growing a Company*; *Leadership Ensemble: Lessons in Collaborative Management from the World's Only Conductorless Orchestra*; *Managing For Dummies*; *The Management Bible*; and *The Complete MBA For Dummies*. For more information, please visit www.petereconomy.com.

Index